CW00827924

Cyber Security

How to Protect Your Digital Life, Avoid Identity Theft, Prevent Extortion, and Secure Your Social Privacy in 2020 and beyond

MATT REYES

Table of Contents

INTRODUCTION

Technology can be a wonderful thing. At its best, it is saving and prolonging lives. Throughout the daily lives of humans worldwide, technology is making their lives easier. The internet and subsequent cybernetic advancements are constantly being uploaded into our daily lives.

A person with heart issues can take an EKG from their phone and print it out on a computer. A businesswoman in America can work with a company in China, without either party ever having to leave their country. Teachers can work with students across the globe through their home computers. Doctors can speak with and in some cases, accurately examine patients from nearly anywhere in the world.

Yes, technology is amazing. In the last two decades, the internet has made globalization and interconnection, across the globe not only possible but fairly commonplace.

Right now, as this is being written, my home is filled with technology that previous generations thought was purely science-fiction. My computer, through which I can conduct video chats with anyone in the world, is essential to my work. My cellphone is often more powerful than my computer and holds many of the same capabilities. My doorbell is part of a security system that I can access remotely, whether I am at home or not. My voice assistant can give a weather prediction, play music, tell a joke, or answer a question, all at the command of my voice.

Exclaiming this even a decade ago would give the impression that I was related to Tony Stark and had some generation of Jarvis connected to my house and mobile devices. Now, though, this selection of devices and many more, are commonplace.

While being able to control all this seems like fun (and it is) people are often unaware of the threats they are inviting into their home.

In the eighties, the fear of technology produced the idea of Big Brother. Basically, people feared that the government was going to spy on them. Whether the common individual had something to hide or not, this was a common issue that plagued the marketers of revolutionary technology.

Today, people connect everything they possibly can to an internet network just so that they can ask Google or Alexa questions and put their lights on voice command. That is a fairly stark contrast from our initial, societal fear. Of course, it makes sense that people fear what they do not understand, so the evolution from conspiracy to convenience makes sense, in theory.

The reality is that people still do not fully understand this technology or how to protect themselves from it. Yet, household technology has become so common-place that people would rather bury their heads in the sands of the "It won't happen to me," desert than secure their home.

HOWEVER...

This guide is not intended to scare you out of using modern technologies. That is nearly impossible. Rather, this guide exists to help you understand the risks and explain how to protect yourself. After all, life is full of risks. Instead of trying to avoid anything with any kind of risk, it is much safer to educate yourself on the risks and how to minimize them.

With that stated, there is a lot to go over, so let's begin!

Chapter 1

INTERNET OF THINGS (IOT)

The Internet of Things commonly referred to as IoT, always seems to be portrayed as something far more complicated than it is. The IoT is described by Webster's Dictionary as, "The networking capability that allows information to be sent to and received from objects and devices (such as fixtures and kitchen appliances) using the Internet."

To simplify and explain that a little more succinctly, IoT is the interconnected devices and appliances within a network. For instance, the Internet of Things in my home, from the introduction would look something like this:

Network Connection

|

Computer   Cellphone(s)   Tablet Smart TV

|

Doorbell- Voice Assistant-Wireless Headphones-
Health Monitor

|

Voice Assistant Mini(s)

Someone else, with a wider network, with more connected objects or "things", might look something like this:

Network Connection

|

Family Cellphones-Computer(s)-Tablet(s)-
Refrigerator-Lights- Thermostat-Smart TV(s)-Vehicle

| | | |

Doorbell- Voice Assistant-Wireless Headphones-
Voice-Activated Remote-GPS-Key Fob

|

Voice Assistant Mini(s)

The IoT is ultimately, anything that can be connected to the internet. However, in terms of Cyber Security, IoT is often used to explain the personal or household network that needs protecting.

This is what the example above illustrates. One person's network is like a single cell in a circulatory system that is always growing. Usually, the Internet of Things that belongs to one household or individual is similar but not completely the same as another household's IoT.

This is an important concept to grasp early on because cybersecurity depends upon the actions that you take to protect your own IoT.

It is also important to note, that the larger and more diverse the person or household IoT becomes, the more susceptible it is to infiltration. That is because not all "things" in an IoT network are created equal. While the connectivity is basically the same, the security of a coffee maker is not going to be as tight as a cellphone.

Example:

Think of it this way: If you have a secret and you tell one person, there is a much smaller chance that your secret will be exposed then if you told five people and much safer than if you told ten people. The reason is not necessarily because you only have one loyal friend. The reason is because the more people that know something, the higher the chances that one of them is going to slip or be overheard. Everyone is different and when you tell that secret to multiple people, it adds variables. The more variables there are, the more vulnerable your secret will be.

The same logic applies to cybersecurity. Hosting a network of appliances on the same network as devices that hold bank information is an odd trend. The reason is that if someone is able to hack into your network, via the virtually non-existent security-enabled refrigerator, they have already broken through the front gates of your digital castle. Now, they are inside your walls and you likely will have no idea until they are able to infiltrate an important device. Even then, they will likely be gone before you realize what was done.

Now, this guide is not intended to take away or make you fear your voice-activated lights. Rather, it is to help you be aware of the potential weaknesses in what you would like to believe is an impenetrable digital fortress. Learning the danger and being aware of it is a pivotal part of protecting yourself from it.

Internet of Everything (IoE)

Internet of Everything (IoE) is often used synonymously with IoT. While that definition is not wrong, exactly, it is incomplete. IoE is in completion, all that is considered IoT, in addition to the data that those "things" collect.

For those of you who have any kind of online marketing knowledge, the additional information that differentiates IoT and IoE is also collected by search engines to make them more relatable. Much like search engines, the more information a content uploader can provide about that content, the more useful that content to the search engine algorithm.

The Internet of Everything not only takes the "things" under its umbrella but also what information they can provide. This will make both the overall IoT, IoE, and humanistic understanding of these "things" more useful.

Ultimately, IoE is what takes the information collected from all of the "things" on IoT and deciphers the usefulness of that data.

We as users of these devices and things are what propagate this data. Our daily interactions, as a society is all being collected and entered into the IoE. All this data is digitized and while it is not specifically targeting anyone, at least on the surface, it is tracking our every move. It knows when we set our alarms in the morning, when our first cup of coffee is ready, and when we leave for work. It knows where we spend our breaks and our lunch and it knows where we shop. Some devices even know what we buy from what store and how frequently we purchase it. (And just think, in the eighties, the only entity the population feared was spying on us was the government.)

Chapter 2

BEWARE OF THESE DANGEROUS WARES

Malware and Ransomware are two of the most popular terms that describe the malicious intent of hackers. These 'wares' are particularly important, because they are commonly used within the cybersecurity sphere. Here is a breakdown of these terms and the danger that they represent to unprotected technology users.

Malware

Malware is any type of malicious bug placed into the computer. Often, malware is programmed to find and exploit weaknesses in a program, software, or device.

According to a <u>McAfee</u> statistic, "Hackers create 300,000 new pieces of malware **daily**."

Daily. That means that there are millions of new malware pieces being created and sent out per month. Due to this volume, it is impossible to know every single category of each and every piece of malware. (Scary, right?) Fortunately, malware pieces often fall into one of these categories:

Adware: Adware is a type of malware that displays unwanted advertisements ad nauseam. While we can all agree that most ads are not welcomed internet content, this is a malicious attack of ads. Often Adware disallows the victim to even use the computer because of all the ads that pop up. What's more, is the frantic attempt to get rid of all the ads can lead the victim to click on something that unwittingly downloads more malware onto the device. (Often, the "No, thank you" option on popup ads have this secondary attack attached to it.)

Bots and Botnets: Bots and Botnets are derived from the word robots. When used for non-nefarious purposes, they can be useful. Often, they are designed to handle monotonous tasks. Yet, when they are created by hackers they are usually a bend of worms and viruses, that often help hackers steal their victim's identity.

Computer Virus: A Computer Virus is a malicious software that infects a device, often without the owner of the device knowing until it is too late. Viruses can be created to do different things throughout the device. It is designed to self-replicate and is always created by a human. However, after it is released, it is self-sufficient. The virus will do what it is designed to do until it is stopped.

Keylogger: Keyloggers, sometimes referred to as a keystroke logger is a surveillance malware. This type of malware records everything that is typed into the computer This includes, but is not limited to:

- Passwords
- Account Numbers
- User Names

- Encryption Codes

Keyloggers are found in both mobile and desktop devices.

Rootkit: Rootkit software allows the hacker to access otherwise inaccessible portions of the infected device. Worse than the gross invasion of privacy, rootkit software is usually unable to be detected. Therefore, hackers can get in, get the information they want and get out without you being any the wiser.

Spyware: Spyware is software that a hacker to retrieve otherwise inaccessible information about their target's computer. The collected information is secretly transmitted back to the hacker via the compromised computer's hard drive. The point of spyware is that the victim does not have any idea their network is compromised.

Trojan: A Trojan is a type of computer virus that is designed to look innocent. However, once it gains access to the device, it wreaks havoc on the system. (Obviously, it was named after the Trojan Horse.)

Worm: Worms, along with Viruses are the most common form of malicious software. A worm works much like a virus, with the same basic abilities. However, a worm does not need a host file. Instead, it can work self-sufficiently, which can make it harder to detect and eradicate.

The unfortunate part about this, is that there are still devices being compromised by these popular malware categories. That is why these remain popular. However, there are steps that you can take to protect your network from being victimized.

Ransomware

Technically, ransomware *is* a type of malware but considering it is becoming the preference of hackers worldwide, this is a threat that needs to be focused on. According to The Cybersecurity and Infrastructure Security Agency (CISA), Ransomware is malware that is created to deny access to a computer system or data until such time as the demand is paid. This is a fairly new and particularly horrific type of malware as it has the power to bring local and larger governments, companies, or other officials to their knees. There is no particular individual that is targeted. As long as the information on the device that is hacked has some kind of sensitive information on it, the hackers might as well have a gold nugget materializing in front of them.

Some of the more widely spread devastation is felt when government, law enforcement agencies, healthcare systems, or other critical infrastructure entities are targeted.

The worst part is, even if the ransom is paid, there is no guarantee that the files will be recovered. Since this crime is such a devastating beast, within the world of cybersecurity, it is difficult to track the hacker responsible. Therefore, many times, the person or people responsible for the ransomware simply disappear with their ill-gotten gains.

Real World Example

NotPetya started in 2017. It was a malicious Ransomware program, developed by Russians. Not long before it, the Petya made its debut a year before but ended up being a parlor trick, compared to its anti-named protege.

Only a few months before, the world had seen WannaCry and even though it did not have the devastating effect of NotPetya, it was a notable ransomware. However, NotPetya ended up being the coup de gras, largely because it was viewed as a cyberattack by factions of the Russian government.

The history of this attack, was that Russia and Ukraine were locked in a war that had lasted a decade. Bloodshed on either side did not seem to make any progress toward winning or losing the war. It was thought that fighting with physical weapons was deadlocking both countries. Therefore, the Russians decided that they needed to introduce a new tactic into the war. Thus, the Ransomware, NotPetya was unleashed on the unsuspecting, war-torn country.

NotPetya encrypted the files of high-profile companies. A few of the victims included TNT Express which is a subsidiary of FedEx, and Maersk. In total, the Ransomware extorted $892.5 million from the companies. The ransomware, once released, spread quickly, demanding Bitcoin payments from companies and turned their systems inside out. TNT Express was reported to still be sorting out the issues a month after the attack.

Prepare

Train Employees Properly in Cybersecurity

Often, the reason for a Ransomware breach is because an employee was tricked into doing something to jeopardize the company's security. However, you do not want to get upset at the employee, because chances are, the employee was never trained to recognize a cybersecurity threat. That is why, as a lead-er or official for your organization it is important to push for the right training. Make sure your employees know the threats that are facing them. Help them understand what a serious risk it poses and why they should be vigilant in keeping the entity safe from a Ransomware attack.

Hire Qualified IT Professionals

There is a lot of crisis that can be averted by hiring the right IT professionals. If the person or people, depending on the size of your IT needs, knows what they are doing, they will be able to take care of a lot of issues, before they become dire. Additionally, they should be able to train employees on cybersecurity safety.

The most important thing, having found a good IT person or team, is to allow them to do their job. Take their advice and while it is never a good idea to blindly follow whatever anyone says, do not ever shut them out. Always remind yourself that you hired them to help you, so let them do what they need to do to keep you, your network, and the information it is responsible for safe from hackers.

Backup Your Files

Files are easy to back up. If there is important information on your computer, you want to ensure nothing happens to it. Therefore, take the time and spend the money to get the right external hard drive to back up the system. That way, if there ever is a threat, you have all the information safely tucked away, where it is ready to be restored when you are sure the threat has passed.

Now, some sneaky hackers will try to lock up your backups as well as your main system. So, to stop them from gaining complete power, you need to make sure your files are safe in multiple locations. In addition to a backup system and external hard drive, put the information on a local system, and a cloud system.

Limit Access to the Information

Limit the access to your network's information by segmenting it into different zones, which require different credentials. Make sure that only certain people in the company have access to the whole network grid. (Namely, a trusted IT employee and perhaps a second in command.) Otherwise, only allow people access to what is pertinent to their particular station.

Doing this makes it much more difficult for one attack to shut down your entire network.

Keep Your Antivirus Software Up to Date

The reason this is said continuously throughout this guide is to help you understand the importance of having antivirus software on your devices. Yes, it is a pain when you have to pay it every year. Yes, it is annoying when you have to unblock websites and other crucial forms of communication for your home or business. Although, if it keeps your devices safe, especially from something as potentially devastating as Ransomware, it is all worth it.

React

According to Statistica, 444,259 ransomware attacks took place worldwide in 2018. The idea that it will not happen to you is a foolish one. With the freedom of information we have and the availability of apps that help people commit these crimes, it is becoming more prevalent in our society. That is why it is important to know what to do and how to react if it happens to you.

Do Not Pay Them

The good thing about information, that is not a factor in having a loved one ransomed, is that information can be copied. If the company keeps a backup of the system, from a certain point, the threat of being held up by ransomware is far less prevalent. Sure, you might end up having to replace computers, which are expensive. Yet, that is the worst case scenario. The actual ransom demand becomes invalid.

Regardless of your preparations, though, the key to keeping your money and your dignity during a ransomware attack is not to pay them. It doesn't matter if the ransom is for $300 like WannaCry was or over $8-Million, like NotPetya. If you give the hackers money you encourage them. There is no one's life on the line. It is just information.

Additionally, as it was stated before, even if you do give them what they want, there is no guarantee you will get your information back.

Whitelist Programs on the Network

Ensure that only select programs are able to run on the network. This will create another barrier for hackers to get through when trying to infect the network. The hard part will be to know exactly which programs should be whitelisted, as many businesses use a lot of different programs. Often, those programs have varying degrees of newness.

Make Use of Your Firewalls

Firewalls are able to block data that is unauthorized from entering the system. There are three main types of firewalls, which each have a different purpose:

- **Packet Filters**- This firewall controls the network access. This is done by the firewall constantly analyzing the outgoing and incoming packets.
  - o "Packets" or Blocks are data that is checked against previously whitelisted data. Examples of this whitelisted data are trusted IP addresses, information nodes, programs and other pre-approved information.

- **Stateful Inspection (SPI)**- This is a more protected firewall, which examines traffic streams from start to finish. Instead of simply looking for similarities new data, comparable to pre-approved data, this firewall analyzes the packets thoroughly, and provides proxy services.

- **Proxy Server Firewalls**-These firewalls are the strongest and are usually reserved for bigger networks. These firewalls inspect incoming data at the application layer. Plus, Proxy firewalls are able to hide your IP address, which makes it easier to limit the types of traffic that even attempt to enter the network.

The first two are better for smaller networks, while the last one is the firewall that is used to secure larger networks. For people who are afraid of a Ransomware attack, though, it is probably a good idea to fortify your network with Proxy Server Firewalls.

Secure

Create a Threat and Response Analysis

After the ransomware threat is secure, it is important to reflect on what worked, what didn't work, and what needs to be added. Cybersecurity for a particular entity can always be improved. See what might help that improvement. If you have different zones for your network, did they work properly? Did the antivirus fail? Was it the firewall that was breached? Or, was it due to human error?

Understanding what went wrong, after the crisis is over can be extremely helpful in patching the vulnerable spots in your network's defenses.

Enable Early Threat Detection

In addition to keeping up to date with antivirus software, there is also ransomware protection that is able to detect potential threats. If you feel as though your business or entity is particularly vulnerable to attacks, you might want to look into this specific type of software.

Run Security Scans

After implementing new security protocols, make sure to run frequent scans to make sure you are able to catch and neutralize threats before they become a problem. Antivirus and even ransomware software is not completely effective unless the network is scanned. Having scans being done in real time can help you recognize potential threats and learn how to react to those threats before there is an emergency.

Chapter 3

COMPUTERS

Computers have completely changed our everyday lives. Personal Computers (PCs) have continued to advance, integrating themselves into our everyday lives. What started as a room full of machinery can now be carried in our pockets. Everything within the IoT and IoE came to fruition because of the creation and evolution of computers. It is truly amazing but the implementation of computers into every aspect of our lives has also made us vulnerable to cyber attacks.

PCs and laptops are still widely used, because mobile technology is still not quite up to the same standards. PCs and laptops still have the most memory and are needed for more complicated tasks. Therefore, they are likely the true target of an attack, because of the extent of information that can be uncovered.

Plus, PCs and laptops are where many people store our pictures, sensitive files, and other personal information. After all, mobile devices can be stolen. Most people do not carry their laptops around with them to high-volume areas, unless it is work or school, so there is less of an opportunity for physical theft.

Yet, there is ample opportunity on PC or laptop for a hacker to find their way into your system.

Real World Example:

While there are plenty of real world examples that made the news, in regard to computer hacks, the Melissa Virus of 1999 was one of the most notable. The reason for this particular virus' infamy was two-fold. First, it was an email virus that was spread through a Microsoft Word Document. Back in 1999, Microsoft was still considered the golden boy of tech, whereas now, the company has some healthy competition. However, the fact that a well-known and trusted Microsoft software was the vehicle that spread the virus, made people extremely leery. The second reason was that the hack was so successful, it infected twenty-percent of the world's computers.

The email came with an attachment, from Microsoft Word with a seductive file name. Once opened, Microsoft Word was compromised, which led to Microsoft Outlook being compromised. From there, the randomized file names would be sent to the victim's first fifty contacts.

The person who was responsible for this hack is named David Lee Smith. (Although, Smith's name is more synonymous with his AOL American Online hack.) However, this attack was far more devastating and ended in Smith being arrested on April 1, 1999 (I'd hate to have to ask someone to bail me out on April Fool's Day!)

Smith plead guilty in December, 1999 and was sentenced in 2002 to a whopping twenty months in Federal Prison and a $5,000 fine. Yet, with Smith's help, cybersecurity was beefed up significantly and people were much wiser to hacker tricks.

Prepare

Install Anti-Virus

Anti-Virus is essential for keeping your computer safe from hackers and the dirty tricks they use to compromise your system. If you do not do ANY-THING else to protect your computer, install anti-virus. It is the last line of defence before a complete takeover. You do not want to leave yourself exposed.

What does Anti-Virus do?

Anit-Virus or Anti-Malware is software that is designed to prevent, detect, and remove malware and other malicious infestations on your computer.

What should I look for in Antivirus software?

There are plenty of antivirus software out there. Companies are creating their own every single day and the companies that are already established work hard to stay ahead of current malware threats. Here are a few things to look for when you are deciding which antivirus to purchase.

Inclusivity: Previously, the different types of malware was discussed and when deciding on an antivirus, all of these types should be taken into consideration. Most reputable antivirus software is good for including protection from most of the common malware threats but do not take that for granted. Make sure you know what your chosen antivirus is protecting you from. Remember, this is not only the cure for many cyberattacks, but also the insurance against it, so be informed.

Compatibility: There are so many devices out there and they all have different years and compatibility requirements. Due to the differentiation in these compatibility requirements, it is essential for you to choose a software that is compatible for all your devices.

Email Scanning: Emails are some of the easiest ways to become the victim of a cyber attack. Phishing scams have evolved with the times and can sometimes seem very convincing. That is why it is important to have backup in case a scam gets through your defenses.

Download Protection: Threats come in all shapes, sizes, and files, which is why it is important for your antivirus to stop any potential threat before it overtakes your computer.

What is the Best Antivirus Software?

1. Norton (LifeLock)
2. Total AV
3. McAfee
4. PC Protect

React

There are several different ways that you can check to see if malware has infected your computer. Here are the most common ways to know that your device is being overrun, before it's too late:

Ads are Everywhere

If ads keep popping up on your screen, no matter where you go or what you do, you are likely experiencing an issue with adware .

Device is Incredibly Slow

Most malware reproduces, like a cancer, growing inside the computer. The more it reproduces, the more memory is being invaded. So, in addition to other attacks, malware often slows your computer down dramatically. (Think dialup, when your sibling kept picking up the phone, just to annoy you.)

Changes to Your Settings

Once malware gets enough control over the infected device, it is likely that certain aspects, like your browser, settings, or even your antivirus software is acting strangely. Keep an eye out for this, as the changes could be subtle at first but eventually, they will be so obvious that you have no choice but to notice. Commonly, new toolbars will show up on your browser and they will not be tools that are of any use to you. Do not click on them. Refrain from exerting your curiosity, it will only end badly.

Online Searches are Redirected

Sure. Everyone has typed the wrong thing into the search bar or forgot to take into account the way they word their search. Whether this is human error or not, we are likely to blame it on autocorrect. However, when you have been hacked, your online searches are redirected to very, very weird places. Chances are, you will immediately know the difference.

Secure

Regardless of who you are or how computer savvy you are, being hacked is a harrowing experience.

Depending on the nature of the hack, you might only have a few moments to react, before your entire network is compromised. Therefore, it is important, in that crucial time period, to follow these steps to mitigate your exposure:

Cut the Strings

If your computer is hacked, the first thing you want to do is isolate your computer from the rest of your network. That way, the malware cannot infect your other devices. Basically, it is the same response the CDC would have upon finding out a person is sick with a foreign agent; they would quarantine them. The way that you do this is to immediately disconnect it from the internet.

In fact, the safest thing to do is to completely disconnect your internet service (pull the plug) and turn off WiFi.

Power Down

Once the internet is no longer connected to your computer, power the computer down. This will make sure that files which haven't been infected yet will remain safe for the time being.

FYI: If you are on a personal network it is extremely unlikely that your computer is able to be rebooted remotely. Once the computer is turned off, if it remains off, the malware cannot infect anything else.

If you are in an office setting, with a network with linked computers, it is possible for a computer to be rebooted remotely. Thankfully, it is still unlikely.

Remove the Hard Drive

The next step is to remove the hard drive from your computer. Connect that hard drive to an alternative PC. Make sure the antivirus on this PC is up to date. Once it is connected, immediately scan your hard drive for malware and other corruption. Use the antivirus software to remove the malware and then back up your files. If you want to keep it, back it up.

Return the Hard Drive

Now, you are able to return the hard drive to the infected computer. Even if a scan tells you that the computer is no longer under attack, DO NOT believe it. Regardless of what the computer tells you, there is no guarantee the malware is completely gone. Not yet, at least.

Wipe the Computer

Use a Secure Disk Erase Utility to completely wipe your computer. This will take everything out of the computer and leave you with a digital shell of a computer. Here are a few of the most popular Secure Disk Erase Utilities:

- PCDiskEraser
- KillDisk
- NWipe
- Eraser

If there is any good news, when it comes to having to wipe your computer, Secure Disk Erase Utilities are one of the few free solutions that are effective and safe.

Reinstall Computer Hardware

Once the computer is completely erased, you need to reinstall the Operating System (OS) and recreating your computer. Yes, it is a long and tedious process, but it needs to be done. Generally, when you buy a device, there is a CD that contains the OS. Use that to return your computer to factory settings and personalize it from there.

Backup Your Computer

Once your computer is back to normal, back it up, so that if anything life this ever happens again, you will not have to reinstall everything piece by piece. Here is how you backup your computer. (With either a PC or a Mac, you can back it up with an external hard drive.)

However, this is how you get to your file backup on the computer itself:

PC:

- Go to your **Start** and choose or type in **Control Panel**.
  - o Click on **System and Security** when the window opens up.
    - ▪ Click on **Backup and Restore**
      - • If this is the first time you are doing this, you are going to have to **Set Up Backup**
        - o Once backup is set up, you are going to follow the onscreen directions that lead you to backing up your files.

Mac:

- Connect your external hard drive
  - o Once the external hard drive is connected, click on the Apple (at the top left of your screen). Find **System Preferences**.

- Once the System Preferences screen loads, find the **Time Machine** option and make sure it is switched on.

  - Select the correct disk (your external hard drive). **Note:** The backup location you choose must be formatted as Mac macOS Extended (Journaled).

    - Once the correct settings are chosen, Time Machine will back up your files.

Chapter 4

WEBCAMS

Webcams were one of the first devices we brought into our homes that had the capability to compromise our cybersecurity. However, at the time, society was so enamored with the ability to talk and see our relatives and friends from the comfort of our own home, that most of us ignored the obvious issue: We were bringing a camera, specifically designed for the internet into our homes. Worse, often the place where the webcam was kept was in a private area of your home, such as a bedroom or office.

In fact, when PCs and laptops started coming with webcams built in, we were practically begging tech companies to take our money. Now, society is still obsessed with webcams, so much so, they are on almost every cell phone on the market.

Cell phones go EVERYWHERE with us and unfortunately, webcams are among the easiest targets for hackers to compromise. There are a few different ways to be hacked, depending on the model of the webcam (or the operating system of your device.)

The first is the scariest: The hacker needs to know the public IP Address of the camera. This horrifically easy method of hacking into a person's webcam came to fruition in 2013 when a list of TRENDnet IP cameras were exposed. A list of leaked public IP addresses were causing cameras to become vulnerable to remote accessibility.

While updates to the software and discontinuation of the affected cameras were put in place, at least five-percent of the cameras were still running as of 2014. Plus, TOR nodes continue to have the capability to scan and access vulnerable cameras to this day.

The second widespread, noteworthy breach happened in 2010, when schools started giving students Mac laptops for their studies. However, what they tried to keep quiet was that there were Remote Administration Tools (accurately named RATs) downloaded on each laptop. Part of these "tools" was called Theft Track and it allowed administration to remotely control the webcam. When this was brought out, the school tried to pass it off as a last resort method of theft protection. However, through the course of a lawsuit, the school admitted that their "last resort" had resulted in 56,000 images of students.

Third, the up to date, current webcams can be accessed through files and is ultimately accomplished through user error. (Sorry.) This is why it is so important to KNOW who you are receiving files from before you open them. Files, usually .scr, .exe, or even a .zip files are used to hide malware. Obviously, the file names seem safe but sometimes, even the information within the file seems safe. That is how some hackers infiltrate the system without the victim having any idea it is happening.

Real World Example

2Channel (2Chan) is a popular online community where people from all over the world share updates, questions and sometimes, live streams. 2Chan originated in Japan in 1999 but has gained notoriety all over the world. Basically, this was a form of a super secret Reddit, before Reddit existed.

In April of 2016, a 2Chan user (who remains anonymous to this day) hacked into **hundreds** of webcams and live streamed their victims through YouTube. What made this even creepier than simply being able to livestream hundreds of people without their knowledge, is this hacker had almost absolute control over their victims' computer. The hacker used this control to make the livestream "interesting". The hacker would cause a freaky image to pop up on the screen when victims got close to their computers and blared music from the victim's PC.

This was certainly a scary case that is made even more unsettling by the fact that the hacker was never identified.

Prepare

Run Your Webcam

If you turn on your webcam and you receive an error message, or you are told that your webcam is already in use, you are likely being hacked.

Cover Your Webcam

If you are using a computer that is not yours, especially a public or RAT device, tape over the webcam lens. That way, even if someone is accessing the webcam, the best they will get is audio.

React

Check Your Lights

When using a webcam or using a device with a webcam, it is important to know what sites you are visiting and what you are receiving. Most webcams have some sort of LED light indicator when it is on. Watch that light and make sure that it is never on when you are not using the webcam.

Find Unknown Applications

Routinely check for unknown applications and files that are downloaded onto your computer. Here is how to do this effectively:

PC:

- Go to your Task Manager:(ctrl+alt+delete) and choose **Task Manager**.
  - Click on More Details when the window opens up.
    - Search the **Apps** and **Background Processes** for anything that doesn't look right. End Task for anything you do not use or do not recognize. (If the process is crucial to your computer,

you will be notified before it is turned off.)

Mac:

- Go to Spotlight:(command+space)
  - Type **Activity Monitor** and hit Enter.
    - Search through **All Processes** for anything that doesn't look right.
      - Select any questionable processes and click "Quit Process". This will prompt a warning dialogue for each process, asking you if you are sure you want to quit that process. Click "Quit" and repeat the process as necessary.

Doing this will get rid of any strange or unwanted apps on your computer and it will also free up space. This will make your computer run faster.

Run a Malware Check

Running a Malware check on your device should be able to isolate any odd files or activity. If it is found, follow the instructions that the malware check gives you. If you do not find it but are sure something is wrong, contact a trusted IT professional immediately.

Secure

Install Malware and Anti-Virus on Your Device

Realistically, this should be the first step when you receive any new device, especially a computer. However, if you do not have malware and/or anti-virus installed, that is going to help salvage your computer, so get it on the device asap.

If you have done all the checks and run the malware and anti-virus without success, it is time to call a professional to look at your computer.

Chapter 5

EMAILS

Emails have revolutionized the way we as humans interact with one another. The discovery and acceptance of emails made the world a smaller place, virtually overnight. Where a letter took a minimum of three days to reach the recipient. A phone call worked better, as you could actually talk to the person but it wasn't conducive to any type of paperwork.

Then, along came emails. This form of communication allowed people to send everything from contracts to images across the world in a few seconds. Emails transformed the entire dynamic of communication. However, as with most amazing technological advances, this came at the cost of our privacy and security.

Where there is a great idea, there is someone out there who is scheming to get rich quick or otherwise do harm with it. That is, unfortunately, how humanity works and emails were ripe for the picking.

Even though we as a society have dealt with Email scammers for more than twenty years at this point, it is alarming to think of how many people still fall for phishing scams. According to Data Connectors, 30% of phishing emails are still opened. Considering all the information that is available about phishing scams, it is hard to imagine that the open rate for emails is so high but considering the age-old list of most popular passwords, it is less difficult to believe.

Email and social networks put us at our most vulnerable. The problem, most of the time is that email phishing scams play with our emotions. Sometimes, they make us fear what we don't understand, while other times, they make us excited. Most people want to believe that awesome experiences can fall into our inbox. Sometimes, they do but more often than not, when such a crazy good email comes through, we know the source. Scammers prey on our impulse emotion and before we know it, we have done something we can't take back.

Fortunately, the more you know about these types of hacks, the more prepared you will be.

Real World Example

Security Intelligence explains a recent phishing scam that had people thinking they were able to go see the World Cup in Russia. This scam emailed victims and informed them that they had won money, lodging, and other prizes. These prizes were supposedly going to be given by the sponsors of the FIFA World Cup.

The emails were accompanied by an attachment or asked potential victims to respond to an address which gave them access to the person's financial records.

Prepare

Secure Your Internet Service

If you have internet at your home, you likely have WiFi that works through a router. While there are other types of internet, this is the most common set-up. It is far less prevalent today than even ten years ago, so chances are, your internet network is secure. This means that you have to put in a password before you can access the internet. This is your network and only people who you give the password to should be able to access it.

If this is not the case, then you are going to get up and secure your internet right now. If you do not know how to do it, you are going to call someone who does. This is not because you are so worried about your neighbors using your WiFi (although, that could be a bad thing, depending on the sites they visit). Many people believe this is the reason that most internet connections are secure. It's not.

If your internet connection is not at least secured, you are basically running a public WiFi network out of your home. This means that even if anyone else is not using it, everything you do on it is vulnerable to attack. Every bill you pay every time you type in a password and every email you send or recieve is being thrown to the digital internet wolves.

Therefore, to avoid risking your financial and personal well being more with every second you have an unsecured connection, put a password on it. Secure your internet service and be thankful nothing horrible happened while it was unsecured.

Do Not Open Suspicious Emails

For anyone who has used email for more than a week, you know who we email and who we use another means of communication with. Some people just love emails but ultimately, emails have become more of a business communication and a place to get coupons. Most personal communication is done over social networks, texting, or even phone calls. So, if you get an email from someone who never emailed you before (and in some cases might not know how to email) be leary of opening something from them. It might not really be an email from someone you know.

Moreover, do not open an email from someone you do not know. Usually, it is incredibly simple to tell whether an email is legitimate or not, without opening it.

If you receive an email that is supposedly from a financial institution, call the institution to see if the email is really from them. Usually, their fraud department will be able to help sort out any questions that you may have. Additionally, if the matter is urgent, especially when it comes to your finances, they probably will not email you. Likely, they will call your phone or send you a letter in the mail. Unless it is something that you are expecting, it is unlikely that their only form of delivery for the news or item is going to be email.

Do Not Open Attachments to Suspicious Emails

Usually, it is the attachments that get you. The email phishing scam is usually a two-step process. The first step is to get you to open the email. That is the canvas through which they paint the emotional picture. Once the email is opened, they can terrify the reader or delight them with their fake promises and claims.

The second step is to get you to open the attachment. Whether this is an image, a file, or supposedly something else, it is the main goal. Once you open that attachment, you are hooked and they are reeling you in.

Use 2-Factor Authorization

Two-Factor Authorization was talked about earlier but this is a good preventative measure, specifically for emails. Many times, emails have extremely private information attached to them, because you believe the information that is being shared is through a private conversation. Usually, this is not a wrong assumption but if a hacker gets into your email, it is no longer a true assumption either.

That is why it is so important to set up two-factor authorization. While it might not save you completely from the nefarious plans of an email account hacker, it will add an extra layer of protection.

React

Change Your Email Password

This is a good idea for any time you suspect your account is compromised. Changing your email password and booting all other devices out of your account will help kick the hacker out so they cannot do any further damage.

Again, when you recreate your email password, make sure it is unique. If it makes sense or you can find it in the dictionary, don't use it. Instead, make it as wacky as possible. The more it doesn't make sense, the better it is.

Inform Your Contacts

If you believe your contacts might be at risk from the breach of your email, tell them about it. You do not want to spread a virus to them in real life, why would you risk them getting a computer virus from your email account? Telling them about the hack is a courtesy thing but it is also to help ensure that the hacker does not get to other people.

Check your Settings

A common theme for hackers is to gain control of your email and adjust your settings so that they receive every email you receive. The scariest part about this type of hack is that the victim does not have any idea. The hacker could be attached to your accounts for an undisclosed amount of time and if you never check your settings, you might never find out.

What do I check my settings for?

Check your settings for anything you do not recognize. If your email is being forwarded to an account you don't recognize, change the setting. If there seems to be anything weird in your settings, you want to get rid of it. Fortunately, it is pretty easy to figure out what each setting means. That makes it easier to figure out what to keep and what to return to default.

Secure

Do Not Give Your Password to Anyone

Why anyone would give their password to someone is something that is not completely understandable. Especially an email password. However, if you have the urge, make sure you fight that urge, because nothing good comes from it. Keep your email your own private communication sanctuary and it will be good to you.

Create an Online Persona

Sometimes, our emails can give away too much. After all, our email goes to everything now. Social media is attached to it, most log-ins require it, and it seems like every time you turn around, you are asked for your email. Therefore, keep yourself separated from your email a little by creating a digital persona. When you create an email, give yourself a name that is different from your own. Make up a birthday and perhaps even change the town where you live. While these are minor changes for adults, that no one is going to care about, they can thwart hacking efforts. Creating an online persona makes it difficult for a hacker to connect the dots of your life and your true identity. That makes it harder to guess passwords and answers to security questions.

Use a Different Email for Social Networks

There are many people who have different email accounts for different purposes. If you have an email account that you use for your personal or work communications, make up a new one for your social network login profiles. That way, your email and your social media accounts will not draw a straight line back to your true identity. After all, there are very few instances where you have actually needed your email for your social networking, besides changing a password.

That way, if either the social network or the email gets hacked, both lines of communication will not be compromised.

Chapter 6

VOICE ASSISTANTS

Google. Alexa. Siri. These are three of the most common voice assistants on the market today. Chances are, you are likely sitting in the same room as one of those voice assistant hubs. If not, your cellphone has a voice assistant. Some televisions and computers are now equipped with voice assistants too.

Voice assistants are helpful and fun to play with. They are helpful for receiving a quick answer to many different questions, ranging from the weather, to an actor's name. These cheerful little voice assistants call you what you want to be called and are always happy to tell you a joke or read your itinerary for the day.

Yet, as we use these little bugs, that we buy with our own money and bring inside our home willingly, it does not occur to most people what they are giving up for instant gratification. It is rare that people ask themselves when they were willing to give up their privacy, simply to be able to ask a robot to play their favorite song.

Sure, there are uses for voice assistants and most of the time, they are harmless. However, they also represent a vulnerability into your home. Voice Assistants are always on. Listening...

Worse yet, these voice assistants are quickly becoming the center of smart homes around the world. In addition to their cute tricks voice assistants can turn on lights and open doors.

And as much as their creators can try to tell us that they are not listening in and that no one else has the capability to listen in, we know it is a lie. However, for the ability to hear a robot call us whatever we want and read us our text messages, we pretend that we believe them.

However, do not be mistaken. There is no fear of the devices themselves. Artificial Intelligence has not reached a level that we have to worry about a Terminator situation or anything. Rather, the enemy that could turn our precious virtual assistants against us are far more familiar than we would like to admit. Human hackers are the real culprits and they have the ability to turn our novelty assistant into a horrifyingly easy to control Brutus; readily helping the hackers destroy the sanctity of our home.

Real World Example

There are plenty of examples of Voice Assistants doing something weird and creepy but as it was previously mentioned, the device itself is not the enemy. Instead, it is the hackers who are going to take advantage of the faults in the voice assistant's programming.

In May of 2018, Daily Mail reported that researchers at the University of California, Berkeley discovered a major vulnerability with virtual assistants. Researchers found that hackers were able to insert secret commands into the transmission signals of the devices. These commands would be recognizable to the devices, thanks to wavelengths, but inaudible to the human ear.

(Imagine being home alone at night. You tell your trusty voice assistant to turn on your favorite song and your door simultaneously unlocks. Or, you wake up one morning, ask your virtual assistant what is on your agenda today and a few minutes later, you receive a receipt for a big ticket item you did not order.)

All this and more, researchers say, can be possible if these vulnerabilities are not rectified.

The flaw reached even the most popular systems, including the three main assistants, Google, Siri, and Alexa.

Prepare

Keep All Your Devices Updated

Updates on all devices can be time-consuming and annoying but it is important to keep your devices up to date to protect against hackers. This is especially true for smart house hubs like your virtual assistants. People do not think about keeping these devices updated, simply because they mostly stay in the background. While they are there when we want them, otherwise, they are quietly waiting.

However, updating software is much more than just adding features. Updates insert patches into areas of vulnerability throughout the system. Additionally, updates change software enough to make it harder for hackers to crack into the updated device.

Turn Off Microphones

While the microphone is a key feature to virtual assistants, there is also a way to turn off the microphone when it is not in use. Utilizing this feature helps to cut any potential evesdroppers out of the conversation, even if your network is compromised.

After all, besides giving commands, if someone is listening to everything you and your family says, they could learn a lot of information about you. Besides the regular numbers and passwords, they can learn about your family; their names, ages, and almost everything there is to know about them. Sadly, this information can be used to convince a family member to get in a car with a stranger, or could be used to play with their emotions, in order to illicit money from anyone in the household.

That is why it is a good idea to turn the microphone off if you are not using it.

Secure Your Internet Connection

Make sure that your internet connection is secure and ensure that the antivirus is working properly. There are a lot of different things that can go awry with your IoT if your internet is not secured. One crack in the armor of your digital security and your life is in the hands of the hacker.

Additionally, getting a VPN is not required for cybersecurity but it also is never a bad idea. It is always a good move to add another layer of protection to your network.

Take Stock of All Your Devices

Over the past few years, the amount of devices that are used in a normal household's IoT has exploded. It is difficult to know exactly what devices are connected. Now, this isn't because we have so many devices we don't know what to do with them. Rather, it is that most individuals take for granted that they have these devices. Even though you might use nearly all your devices every day, you don't think about their classification, so sometimes that takes some cognitive effort.

Once you have all of your devices accounted for, though, you can make sure that they are getting updated properly.

React

Shut Down the System

Once you realize you are hacked, it is extremely important to shut off the access point. If you believe your virtual assistant is the problem, turn it off. Fortunately, a virtual assistant is still something that you can just unplug. However, unplugging the virtual assistant might not ensure the hacker is booted out of the system. Thus, it is important to shut down your network until you can figure out what is compromised and eradicate it.

Talk to Family Members

Explain the situation to family members within the household. While you cannot expect everyone to remember what they said in their own house within the past few weeks, you can warn them. Explain that there might have been a breach and someone might have overheard something personal. Assure them that this is not meant to scare them. Rather, it is meant to inform them and bring their attention to the fact that someone could say something, in person, by phone, over email, or over messenger that is extremely personal. Get them to understand that they should not believe them and if it is about another family member, the first thing they should do is get in touch with that family member.

For households with small children, this is the time to reinforce stranger danger. Explain that there is absolutely no reason a family member would send a stranger to pick them up, no matter what they know.

Wipe the Devices

After ensuring that the breach was dealt with and doing a malware scan, you are going to want to restore the device to its factory settings. Change all names and passwords connected to the device and pretend that the device is brand new. This is the next best thing to actually getting brand new devices.

Secure

Keep Certain Smart Features Separate

Do not give your virtual assistant so much power. Of course, it is okay for your virtual assistant to turn on lights or turn off the television. However, maybe it is not a great idea to give the assistant access to your door locks. This is especially true if a breach has already happened. There is no harm in having smart locks, alarms toasters, coffee makers, thermostats, thermometers, lights, and garage door openers. However, it is a good idea, from a cybersecurity perspective to keep certain smart gadgets away from the all-inclusive hub that is so easy center around a virtual assistant.

Do Not Give Virtual Assistants Sensitive Information

Virtual Assistants are glorified filing cabinets (or databases, if you'd rather) with internet capabilities. That is it. The insecurity comes with the knowledge that they can be hacked and they are a part of the internet. Therefore, it is important that you do not provide this potentially vulnerable filing cabinet with information that you wouldn't tell a friend. Do not give your virtual assistants your bank number, your pin number, your social security number, or your passwords.

Divulging this information to a device, simply so that it can remind you at a later date is simply irresponsible. It is asking for trouble.

Chapter 7

KEY FOBS

Imagine, hearing a car rev to life in your driveway. At first, you think your significant other is home early, or you have a visitor. When you do not hear the normal sounds that accompany these everyday occurrences, you look out the window to check. To your surprise and horror, you see a person you do not know backing out of your driveway, with YOUR CAR and speeding away.

Chances are, you are stunned for a moment but your first logical thought is that you must have left the car unlocked with the keys inside. However, a second wave of shock hits you when you see your key fob hanging on the hook by the front door.

Sadly, keyless entry key fobs and the cars that have this feature have produced a new vehicle for nearly effortless car theft. Now, with a strange looking device, implements a quick and efficient SARA or Signal Amplification Relay Attack.

Real World Example

October of 2018 was not a good month for a Tesla Model S car owner, as he was the victim of a car theft, conducted via a Signal Amplification Relay Attack. This poor person's car was stolen right from his driveway.

Did he leave his keys in his car? No. They were hanging on a hook, inside his home. This is a scary attack, because the video of the car being stolen is so quick and seemingly easy, that it is no wonder this is becoming a growing concern for car owners.

The only hiccup in the plan had nothing to do with the hack, or the actual theft. Ironically, it turned out that the best security the car had against these thieves was the plug that charges the car.

Unfortunately, the thieves were far more tech savvy than their plug debacle suggests because they knew to remove the SIM card from the vehicle. This makes the car unable to be tracked by GPS.

Prepare

Keep Your Key Fob in a Can

There are many different more *ahem* technical security measures that can be taken to ensure your key fob car is not stolen via this hack. However, even after implementing all of them, according to Moshe Shlisel, CEO of GuardKnox Cyber Technologies. "Really, some cyber experts don't go to sleep without putting their key into a metal container. It's called a Faraday Cage. You block the electromagnetic field."

However, a can by any other name, is still a can and it is one of the most effective defenses against modern car theft.

Use The Anti-Theft Technology

Okay, so if you are going to drop a small fortune on a Tesla, or if you are going to buy a car in general, it makes sense to use the anti-theft technology. The criminals in the real world example above were extremely lucky, because the owner failed to enact the built in safety features that the car has.

The car in question and likely most cars of this caliber have the option to put a pin into the touchscreen to make the car start after the key fob unlocks the door. The owner did not bother to do that.

The car also has the option to turn off keyless entry. This is actually recommended by Tesla. Obviously, the previous owner of that beautiful car didn't do that either.

While anti-theft technology does not absolutely secure your vehicle from being stolen, it sure helps make it more difficult to steal!

Secure your Vehicle in a Garage

Seriously. If you have access to a garage and you intend to leave it somewhere overnight, put it in the garage, or behind a gate, an invisible fence...something! Gone are the days when you have to make a lot of noise to steal a car. Physical skill and finesse is being replaced by one-hit wonder technology.

At least, right now, key fobs are pretty much all created equal. Thus, if the signal can be interrupted in one key fob, it is possible to interrupt other key fobs. With this in mind, it is a good idea to put other barriers in the way, that are not reliant on the car.

React

Car theft is a scary thought but we live with the reality of a possible car theft every day. Unfortunately, instead of making your car safer, many people choose to ignore the risk. Sure, you may take precautions against the car being stolen but besides anti-theft technology, there is not much else that is done. Here is what to do if your car is stolen:

Report the Theft

Whether your car is an old beater, or a Tesla, if your car is stolen, you need to report the theft. Make sure you have your license plate number and VIN number handy as well. Make sure to provide a good description of the car and any discerning features it has. The sooner you report the theft, the sooner police can start tracking the car.

Pull Up GPS of the Car

There are a lot of newer cars that are equipped with GPS. Access the GPS in the car as soon as you realize it is missing. This could prove to be vital in tracking down the car. Chances are, if the car has a keyless entry system, it has a GPS.

It is also a good idea to make sure you know how to pull up the GPS in the car before the car is actually stolen. That way, you do not have to figure anything out while you are freaking out because someone just drove off with your car.

Submit an Insurance Claim within 24 Hours

Unfortunately, if your car is stolen, it is unlikely it is going to be returned to you. Thus, it is important to file a claim with your insurance company as soon as possible. Of course, try everything you can to get your car back. Still, you will know, well within that twenty-four hour window if your car is likely to be recovered or not.

Secure

Install a Killswitch

Chances are, if your car is stolen or if there is a close call, you are going to want to do everything in your power so that it never happens again. This is where a killswitch comes in. A killswitch is also an extra GPS tracking device, which can be installed behind the dashboard. If the car is stolen, you can locate the car and turn it off with the killswitch, so that police can move in. (Yes, police. You do not want to put yourself in peril by trying to handle this yourself.)

This extra piece of self-assurance will come in handy if the thieves disable or remove the car's factory GPS.

Prepare a List of Valuables

People leave all different things in their cars. One thing people do not think about is if their car is stolen, so are all those valuables. If something does happen to the car, even if you get it back, you are going to want to know what was in there. That is why it is a good idea to write out a list of valuables that are kept in your car and keep it in a safe place. (Not in the car.) That way, again, during the hectic scramble and wild emotions of an emergency, you do not have to think about what valuables you are missing. You will be able to give insurance a list that was compiled when you were able to think clearly.

Chapter 8

SECURITY SYSTEMS

Security systems are meant to make people feel safe. While security systems have been around for many years, with varying degrees of complexity, more people have them now, than ever. This is thanks to IoT and the connection that you have to digitized, internet based 'security'.

To be fair, both wireless security systems and surveillance systems, which will be talked about later, have done their duty, keeping people safe. However we cannot take the idealistic intentions of anything throughout the IoT for granted. After all, it can be hacked and thus, anything it does for us can also be done to us.

Real World Example

A couple in <u>Wisconsin</u> thought they were being cautious when they installed a $700 security system in their home. All was well for a few days but then, one afternoon, the woman came home to find that their house was 90 degrees. The security system was connected to the thermostat and the doorbell.

Thinking that it was just a new system, the woman summed it up to being a glitch. However, it was way worse than that. Soon after the first attack, a hacker would reveal themselves. The couple claimed that the hacker spoke to them through their security system and played vulgar music throughout their home.

The couple claimed that it was a nightmare and when they contacted the company behind the system, the representative insisted that there was not a breach.

Cybersecurity experts claim that once a system is taken over, they can unlock doors and completely take your home over. When that happens, there is no escape.

Do Not Tell Your Friends Your Security Code

This seems innocent enough. People are watching your house or feeding your dogs while you are away. The easiest way for them to get in or out is for you to tell them your security code. Then, a year or two later, you have a falling out. Guess what? Now a potential enemy has everything they need to get into your home. Whether they would do it or not depends on the person. However, people do some really crazy things, especially when they are angry. (This goes for girlfriends and boyfriends too!)

If you must give out your code, whenever you come back from vacation, or if you and your significant other have a fight, change the code. That way, you can rest assured that you are safe, at least from an easy crime of opportunity.

Prepare

Isolate your Security System

The more that is attached to your network, the more compromisable it can be. If you isolate the network that your security system works off of, it needs to be hacked, but it does not affect anything else. That means that the hackers could turn off your alarm but they will not be able to open doors or have access to the rest of your household IoT devices.

Keep Your Antivirus and Firewalls Up to Date

Letting anything in the cybersecurity sphere lax into even minimal obsoletion can put you at risk. That is why it is always important to keep everything updated appropriately. Remember, hackers look for unpatched gateways and vulnerabilities in the system. By not updating your systems, it is making it easier for them to break in.

Secure Your Mobile Phone

Many of the wireless security systems available are connected to mobile phone applications. So, keeping your mobile phone up to date and secure, you are also keeping your security system secure. Much like the antivirus and firewalls, if your mobile device has a weakness, you can be sure that a hacker is going to use it to their advantage.

React

Take Your Security System Offline

If your security system is being used against you, the first thing you are going to want to do is cut of the head of the snake. Take your security system offline. Turn everything off. That way, the hacker does not have any further direct access to you and if they did put any malware on your system, it cannot continue to corrupt it.

Run a Malware Scan

Run a malware scan. Hopefully, this will pinpoint the breach so that you can get rid of the issue. Although, if the scan comes up with nothing, you are going to want to wipe your system. After all, if your security system is hacked, there is something severely wrong, whether the scan tells you so or not.

Change Your Passwords

Changing your password is usually the first step. Although, if the hacker is going after your security system, if you change your password it isn't going to do much, as the hacker might still be able to see what you are doing. Yet, after you are sure the hacker is booted out of the system, malware and all, you need to change your passwords. Do not make them anything like the passwords you had before. If the hacker figured them out before, a variation of the same password is not going to pose much of a challenge.

Secure

Selectively Authorize Apps and Devices

If you have to put your security system on the same network as your other devices, be selective of the power you give them. Deactivate anything you do not use and update frequently. Do not give permission for your social networks, email, and other highly unstable entities to have unfettered access to the network. Additionally, do not allow all of your devices, including lights, thermostats, and locks to all have free access to your network.

Use Zones for Your Home

Business use zones so that only certain people can access portions of the network. This is also done to create an extra level of cybersecurity. However, this process can be helpful for a home, too. Instead of maintaining more than one network, zone the network off, so that there are barriers, or firewalls, set up between important data and the outside world.

Keep Sensitive Data Off the Network

The old adage, do not put all your eggs in one basket may not traditionally relate to cybersecurity, but it certainly does help this analogy. Your home is generally where everything you love lives and is kept. Your family lives there, your belongings are there, and everything you work hard to maintain is usually under that roof. However, when it comes to the data and devices that protect that home, you do not want to keep all of those "eggs" in one network "basket". After all, devices, from a hacker point of view are useless if they do not have the right data. If they cannot figure out that data, or find it somewhere on the network, then the hack has failed. So, do not put sensitive data on the network, to be used to destroy your life further, should you be hacked.

Chapter 9

SURVEILLANCE SYSTEM

A few short years ago, when someone thought of a surveillance system, they thought of a mansion, with cameras surrounding the perimeter. Having a surveillance system either meant you were a household living on the upper-crust, or you had something to hide. In movies, surveillance systems are either in wealthy homes (usually of the villian) or they are the result of a paranoid genius, hacker, or otherwise computer savvy individual.

I guess it wouldn't be very dramatic, though, for people to walk up to a Ring or Google Nest and speak to their person of interest through the device in a suburban neighborhood. This is especially true when it is obvious that having such a surveillance system is becoming more and more routine.

Now, average, every-day people have the ability to look at their phone and see who or what is at their door, from across the world. This is amazing to most and gives a sense of complete security.

However, considering what these people see on these devices, it makes us leery of exactly what we have been missing, going on right outside our door. Sometimes, it even makes us wish we didn't know.

Yet, since the Ring, Google Nest, and other similar surveillance systems are technology, they can be hacked. This means that it is a real possibility that while you are doing everything you can to protect your family, someone is watching their every move without you having any idea.

Real World Example

A couple in <u>Illinois</u> received the shock of their life, late in 2018 when they heard a man speaking to their baby through their surveillance system. Not knowing what it was at first, the baby's father rushed into the room but could not find anyone there. Originally, the couple thought it was a malfunction of the baby monitor. However, when it happened again, the man was screaming obscenities at the child.

It is horrifying enough to know that someone is watching you but when a stranger is watching and interacting with your child, that adds a whole new level of creep to the situation. Fortunately, the couple rectified the situation and the child is okay. Yet, the parents will be forever scarred by the incident and leery of what they bring into their home.

Prepare

When it comes to surveillance cameras, the unfortunate part is that people set up these systems to ensure no one is getting close to their family. Yet, when these systems get hacked, they are the ones that are being watched.

Having a hack like this infiltrate your life, even if no one steps inside your doorway physically, it destroys the sanctity of your home. So, take every precaution before you get hacked. Here are a few of the best preparations:

Encrypt Your Signals

Use a VPN or other form of encryption to add an extra layer of protection to your security cameras. Make sure that you watch any alerts you receive carefully and take any threats to your cybersecurity seriously. Encryption does not put your home in a bubble, but it certainly builds a moat around your home. It is going to make it much more difficult for someone to get into your system, especially without you knowing. This is what you want.

Take Traditional Safety Precautions

Always lock your doors and windows. Even though you have security cameras, it doesn't mean that you should forgo the age-old safety precautions we all grew up with. Digital systems can malfunction and of course, they can be hacked. If you lock a door or a window, it is locked.

Even locking interior doors at night will help put another barrier between you and an intruder. After all, having cameras does not guarantee that home invasions will not happen. You need to marry digital and physical deterrents throughout your security network to make yourself and your home as safe as possible.

Secure Your Devices

In addition to encryption, always make sure your data is secured and is staying updated. Even if your devices are encrypted, if the updates are not keeping the device relevant, you might as well not have anything. Insufficiently updated devices are worthless and what's scarier, is they will give you a false sense of security.

React

The sooner you react to being hacked, the easier it will be to shut the hack down and the less information the hacker will obtain. However, first, you need to know you are being hacked. So, here are a few abnormalities that are sure to give the presence of a hacker away.

Listen for Any Odd Noise

If a network is uncompromised, you shouldn't hear anything strange. However, if someone is playing around in your system, they are likely to make noise. Depending on what they are hacking, you may hear them, either in-person or on the recording of your feed. Do not rationalize odd noises. Nobody wants to face the reality that they are being hacked but it can be dangerous to rationalize early signs of a hack away. So, if you hear a weird noise, do not assume you are hearing things. Unfortunately, it is safer to assume the worst and ensure that you get to the bottom of it.

Camera Rotates or is Set at a Weird Angle

People with a security system look at their cameras on a daily basis. Even if there is nothing wrong, everyday occurrences set off the sensor. Thus, most people are used to the angle of their cameras. So, if that angle changes, homeowners need to figure out why. Cameras do not just move on their own. So, if you didn't move it, who did? If you don't know, you should assume that you have been hacked.

Watch Your Data Usage

Nowadays, many people have unlimited data, so it is no longer necessary for you to watch your usage like a hawk. Back before unlimited data became the norm, people would notice any spike in their data but now, a lot of people might not even know where to check for it. However, from a cybersecurity standpoint it is vital to not only know where the data is recorded, but how much is normal. If you look at your data and see a spike, that might mean that someone else has joined the network.

Secure

Check Your Feeds

Sometimes it is hard to tell if the camera moves. (Some people have cameras that are motion-sensored, after all.) So, a good way to make sure your cameras are not being controlled remotely is to check your feed. Most feeds have the IP address of the computer accessing it. If you check your feed and notice a different IP address, you might have a problem.

Note: You don't have to know your IP address. Generally, the same number will be attached to most of the feeds. When that number differs at all, it is time to do a little more investigating.

Turn Off the Option to View Remotely

While this feature can be nice for viewing what is going on while you are at work, or otherwise away from your house, it can also be a port of entry for a hacker. So, unless it is absolutely necessary, it is a good idea to only be able to view the feed while you are home, accessing your own WiFi network, with all the comforts and protections that come with it.

Chapter 10

SMARTPHONES

Out of all the people in the world, in 2019, 66.53% (roughly 5.13 BILLION) of those people have a mobile device, according to Bank My Cell. However, you probably didn't need a statistic to prove how widespread mobile technology has become.

For most people around the globe, it is now difficult to find an adult without a cellphone. While the smartphone penetration, across the worldwide market is still developing, it is still not overly difficult to find a person with a smartphone.

Many people have allowed mobile devices to infiltrate every aspect of their life. For many, being connected to their friends and family via a mobile device allows them a sense of security. Plus, the endless amount of entertainment that mobile devices, smartphones especially, provide make it difficult for you to be bored.

We take our cell phones everywhere with us. They are the one thing that people do not leave the house without and never part with. Many of us don't even go to the bathroom without our pocket-size connection to the outside world.

However, what many people do not realize is that our coveted protection and connection device can become a demonspawn if it is hacked.

Real World Example

This real world example is kind of an odd one, as it has allegedly gone on since 2005. Or, at least, that is when the world first caught on. The UK Phone Hacking Scandal accuses journalists of paying police to help them hack into phones of celebrities, the Royal Family, lawyers, and even murder victims.

This all started in 2005 when News of the World (NoW) broke the story of Prince William injuring his knee. The royal family immediately suspected what was going on. They alleged that police had helped NoW journalists hack into the Prince's phone. After an investigation, however, NoW is absolved of suspicion, but the complaints continue to come in.

After some back and forth and finally, an admission/apology from NoW, the suspicions are proven true. This is in large part thanks to former NoW journalist Sean Hoare spilling the beans in his allegation, which forced the newspaper's hand.

However, even after the admittance and apology, NoW was still being accused of hacking noteworthy phones throughout Britain. However, the most deplorable allegation comes from the family of Milly Dowler. Milly Dowler was abducted and killed by a serial killer, Levi Bellfield in 2002. Milly's family alleges that NoW hacked into her phone and erased messages off her voicemail after she disappeared. Wanting to believe there was still a chance Milly would be found alive, the family clung to the deletion of the voicemails as hope that she was still alive. Although, finding out that Milly was sadly, no longer alive resulted in NoW journalists having a lot to answer for.

Even in February of 2019, the lawyers of celebrities such as Elton John, David Furnish, Elizabeth Hurley, Heather Mills, and Fiona Mills have released statements saying they have settled lawsuits with NoW over the hacking of their clients' devices.

Prepare

Update! Update! Update!

Trust me, nobody likes to go through the inconvenience of updating their mobile device. Those ten minutes without it can seem like an eternity. Then, when your connection to the outside world is finally returned to you, the interface has changed. Learning where everything is again and getting used to finding your most-used apps quickly takes more time than anyone wants to spend. This is only for you to learn the new interface, just in time for another update.

However, updating your device is extremely important. It ensures that the latest firewalls are installed and patches are made to the device. Keeping your device updated with the newest software ensures reliability, speed, and safety. After all, if your annoyed at having to figure out a slightly different interface, imagine what it is doing to mess up a hacker's stride.

Two-Factor Identification is the Key

Again, I know. When you're in a hurry and your trying to access something on your device and a two-factor identification notification pops up. (It happens at the worst time, amiright?) *Ugh.*

So, then you have to pull out your other device...and sometimes it takes a few minutes (that feels like hours) to send the notification and then...it times out.

Seriously, two-factor identification definitely has its...annoyances. However, it is a good way to ensure you are the one who is waiting over the mobile phone, waiting for the ability to unlock your other device. Part of the reason it works so well is because it is annoying. For most hackers, it wouldn't be worth the trouble. Therefore, it is definitely worth waiting those few extra minutes, to ensure your own security.

Don't Bait a Hacker with Your Screen Lock Notifications

It might sound silly, being leery of what your lock screen notifications reveal. However, it is one of those freaky things that seems harmless, until it isn't. For instance, if you work as a bank manager or at a place where there is a lot of sensitive information stored, your notifications could give that away. For instance, pretend "Tom" works with you and you have a meeting tomorrow. He texts you, innocently enough, and it shows up like this:

Tom- "Name of" Bank- *Don't forget to bring the coffee for the meeting tomorrow. I just picked up the donuts.*

If someone sees that notification while you are out in public, they will know you have a meeting at a bank tomorrow. Logic will help them assume that if you are bringing coffee, you probably work at the bank. If you work at the bank, you might have information on your phone that might help them siphon money out of that bank. So, they take your phone or worse, clone your phone.

Again, this might seem far-fetched but there are plenty of common situations where something like this can happen and hackers can take advantage.

Lock Your Apps Up!

This one might also be good for if your children play with your phone but it is also adds an extra layer of security. Both Android and iOS operating systems have the capability to lock certain apps up, in addition to locking your phone. That way, even if a hacker got into your phone, you would at least have some time to react before they had access to ALL of your sensitive data.

React

When a mobile device is compromised, reacting quickly and efficiently is the best way to ensure the safety of your information. Depending on the sensitivity of the information that is on the hacked or stolen device, the severity in your options are definitely ranged. Here are the options when it comes to reacting to a hack or realizing your device was stolen (or even lost).

Track your Phone

Phone tracking has been around for both Android and iOS operating systems for a while now. While this is convenient for those who are forgetful, it is indispensable when your phone is stolen. Both Apple and Android have their own respective "Find My Phone" settings. Once this setting is enabled or downloaded, depending on the mobile device, the phone can be pinpointed on a map if it is lost. That can help you retrieve your phone, hopefully before it becomes fully compromised.

Erase Your Phone

For those of you who are extremely worried about the data on your phone being exploited, there is an option to erase the contents of the device. This can be initiated after a certain amount of wrong passwords are entered. Or, if that seems like it might be at your own digital peril, you can track your phone and erase it remotely.

Use Your Smartwatch

Android and iOS have a plethora of smartwatches that are compatible with a range of devices. It is pretty amazing what these watches can do by themselves, let alone with the help of a device.

However, in addition to looking like Maxwell Smart or, if you prefer, Inspector Gadget, a smartwatch is also a handy defense against thieves. Many smart-watches inform you when your phone has disconnected from your watch. If that notification comes to you while you are in a public place, there is likely an issue. Yet, when you get the notification, the phone cannot be more than 50 feet away. So, if you call it, there is a good chance you will catch the culprit.

Secure

Install Antivirus on Your Device

Generally, if you have antivirus on your PC, you will also have the ability to install it on your phone. Most antivirus providers now come with the capability of accommodating a plethora of different devices.

Get Rid of Weird Apps

Mobile devices can sometimes be corrupted by a single app that is placed on the phone. In some cases, when that app is deleted, the phone is cured. While it sounds easy, this could be a more harrowing process than you might originally think. Most people have a lot of apps on their phones. Even moderately cyber-security conscientious people fall for downloading apps on a whim. While most of the time it is fine, sometimes, you download a diseased app.

That is why it is important to go through all of your apps and see if anything weird is going on. Is there an app that is using more data than its supposed to? Was an app updated recently?

Updates, while they are excellent when they are coming from reputable sources, can also be the gate through which malware can enter. While most apps wouldn't dare jeopardize their reputation, there are some apps that are innocent at first but turn nasty after a few updates. After all, you have already downloaded it, so most people do not think twice about allowing an app to update.

And that is when they strike.

Restore Your Phone to Factory Settings

This is the last thing you want to do because it will take all of your personal information off the device, along with the malware. On the plus side, much like wiping a PC or laptop, this is a good way to ensure the malware is completely eradicated. Yet, a factory reset means that the phone will return to the state it was in when you first got it. While contacts and pictures can usually be salvaged before the reset, text messages, most apps, and personalized settings will be erased.

Chapter 11

SOCIAL MEDIA

Social media is an interesting concept. It is so popular, with many different platforms popping up all over the place. People love to share what they're doing, how they're feeling, and other overly private information. Yet, they wonder why they have no privacy.

Granted, social media does have its uses and undoubtedly, it is fun to scroll through news feeds but from a cybersecurity standpoint, it is overly intrusive. Social media takes airing laundry, feuds, personal details, and even TMI moments to the extreme.

That being said, there are ways to keep yourself safe on social media and still enjoy your newsfeed uninhibited. Here is a breakdown of some of the most popular social media sites and subsequent safety concerns.

Facebook

Why do we love Facebook so much? After all, this was the specific platform that gave our information to marketers for years. Not only did they collect information on us, they straight up sold it. What did we as a Facebook loving society do? We treated Facebook like the prodigal son and forgave it for its transgressions. Sure, there was a small boycott facebook movement that lasted a couple of days. Yet, somehow, we just couldn't find it in our social media loving hearts to stay mad at the frat boy, turned rich thief and his cohort of a platform. We took them both back with open arms and there are still millions of people who use Facebook daily.

Security Dangers of Facebook

Privacy

Unfortunately, when it comes to privacy, Facebook does not have the best track record. People who use their "privacy" settings have to fix the settings every time there is an update on the Facebook system. The simple explanation is that every time Facebook goes through an update, all the settings are switched back to default (a public profile, essentially). The main issue with this is that people might not even know that the switch has happened. So, while Facebook privacy can be a good thing, it is important to keep on top of it, because Facebook doesn't care about your privacy.

Scammers

Scammers are all over Facebook. The nist common way that scammers try to hack into your system is through your friends. They use their name and any profile information they can get to send you messages and emails. One of the most prolific scams through Facebook is called the 419 Scam. This scam would send potential victims a message "from your friend" explaining that they were mugged, hurt, and in need of money. Of course, upon getting this message from who people thought was their friends, emotion took over. Many people were victims of this scam because their concern for their friend overrode their scam alert sensors.

Another way that scammers get to people on Facebook is to make their own, fake profile. According to CNet, "Facebook estimates that about 3 percent to 4 percent of accounts on the website are fake."

With these fake profiles, hackers will befriend you and follow your posts. If you post something that indicates you will be away, they could take the opportunity to rob you. Or, if you give out any other information, hackers will find a way to use seemingly innocent information against you.

Keeping Yourself Protected

While Facebook may hold no regard for your safety and protection from hackers while using their service. However, that certainly doesn't mean that you should follow their lead. Thankfully, there are a few different ways that you can keep yourself safe and still enjoy the platform.

Logging In

The ability to log into your Facebook is the quickest way for a hacker to destroy your digital life online. Therefore, it is important to secure anything that can be used to crack into your login information.

The most important thing, besides having a long, nonsensical password is hiding your email address. While an email address is something that you give away rather freely, you still do not random strangers having access to it without you being aware. Thus, it is important that you hide it on your profile. Here is how to do that:

- Log into Your **About Me** page

- o Find the **Contact and Basic Info** option in the left-hand column
  - ▪ Hover over the **Email** option and click **Edit** when it shows up.
    - • Hit the first **Down Arrow** on the right hand side.
      - o Select **Only Me.**

Do Not Save Your Password on Public Computers

This is another safety tip that seems obvious but sometimes, people do not pay attention to what they are doing or they forget they are on a public device. However, it is important to remember, when you are accessing the internet in any capacity, you are open-ing yourself up to the world. If you are using a public computer, the risk is even greater because you are not in your own element. You have no way of really knowing what kind of protection the device has or what other people are using the device. That is why it is imperative that you never save your passwords on a public computer. Plus, you must always log out of your accounts before leaving the computer.

Keep an Eye on Your Friend's List

Too many people have a habit of simply adding anyone who requests them on Facebook. While this could be a good way to gain followers, it is a great way to get scammed or hacked. Of course, many people have a large online presence and might not know everyone that friend requests them personally. While it is not a good idea to ever add random strangers, if you feel your reasoning is good enough, then please take this precaution: Look at their profile page. Was this page just created? Is there nothing more than a profile picture? If this is the case, this is a dummy profile and you do not want to allow it access to your newsfeed. If you do not know someone, make sure there profile has realistic history before adding them.

Twitter

Twitter can be a place for plenty of opportunity and information. Sometimes, it is even the go-to place for hard news, that is still being uncovered. It can be an extremely useful resource for hobbies, work and other areas of interest. However, Twitter is a place where people are more relaxed about their friends and followers. While Facebook is more geared toward friends, Twitter is more of a common celebrity type of platform. People do not usually go to Twitter to keep track of their real life friends and family. Rather, they go on to post and read witty one-liners or get quick information about a variation of topics.

There is nothing wrong with this, as this behavior is how we have allowed Twitter to evolve, as users. Many times, even though the people are virtually strangers, the Twitter community is extremely supportive. Twitter can be really fun. Yet, it is always important to remember that you are still online. Therefore, you should always be concerned about your safety and security.

Security Dangers of Twitter

Fast Information

It is always nice to have a plethora of information in small, bite-sized pieces, hand-fed to you. Twitter is really, really good at that. With the character limit on a Twitter post, people are forced to get to the point much quicker than on any other platform. It is also a great way for the message you put out on the internet to get seen, quick.

These restrictions also force Twitter users to be creative. While creativity is something we generally have to search for in our society now, Twitter makes it a necessity. The security issue is that people might not say exactly what they mean. Or, even if they do mean exactly what they say, the world will hear it and judge it long before you have a chance to clarify your point.

Recently, there were a lot of celebrities that got in trouble for posts they made on Twitter years ago. However, one current misunderstanding could spread like wild-fire and get you into even more trouble.

Thus, it is always important to think about what you post on Twitter, because once it is Tweeted, it can never be fully retracted.

Faux Twitter

The threat of landing on the wrong website, or a faux website, (basically a hacker's playground) is not new. It is, however, still a terrifying tool that scammers and hackers use to solicit personal information from unsuspecting users. Twitter is a common website that can be compromised.

Always make sure the URL to Twitter is Twitter.com. One letter variation, missing or otherwise could lore you into a security-risk trap. Even if the information you "Tweet" on a website like this might not be revealing, interacting with the faux Twitter at all could be opening a door into your personal information.

Therefore, always make sure the Twitter you are using is the Real Twitter. Otherwise, there is no telling what kind of hacking rabbit hole you could fall down.

Keeping Yourself Protected

Twitter can be an extremely useful resource. Although, it can only continue to be useful if you use it wisely. While Twitter does not have such a blatant disregard for your privacy, like Facebook, it isn't any better. In fact, it is easier to be anonymous on Twitter than on any other platform. Since Twitter is mostly just words and does not have a strict profile policy, you can be whoever you want on Twitter.

And if you can achieve this level of anonymity, it's scary to think what kind of havoc a hacker can wreak. That is why it is super important to keep yourself protected while using Twitter.

Location, Location, Location

Twitter users have gotten into the strange habit of telling their "followers" everything they are doing, all the time. This ranges from bathroom habits, to vacations and most of the time, the people who are used to such an invasion of privacy think nothing of giving their current location.

After all, most believe it is a small price to pay for the internet fame that they receive from managing such an active account. What they don't know, though, is that this could be a horrifically bad idea and they wouldn't have any idea, until it was too late.

Telling a social networking account, with thousands of followers that you are on vacation alerts people that you are not home. If they follow you, they have access to your previous tweets, where there is likely more information about your home. (Pictures and other evidence that could work against your privacy.) This makes it very easy for followers to find your home and burglarize it.

Or, possibly worse, if you mistakenly tell your followers that you are home alone.

To mitigate this security risk, post pictures and witty posts about your vacation when you are back home. Or, if you are home alone, wait until you are no longer home alone and post that creepy happening, or baking fail. Don't give that many people real-time information that could some way put yourself in jeopardy.

SnapChat

Sometimes people have an idea and in an idealistic world, that idea is a good one. Although, when the idea is introduced to the real world, immediate problems arise. While this is unfortunate, we cannot will the real world to become intrinsically good-intentioned. Therefore, an app like SnapChat is inherently dangerous, from a security point of view.

SnapChat was designed to be able to share a moment, with "real" friends. It is a direct communication app, where people can send messages to groups or individuals, sharing whatever is happening in their lives. Then, unless a screenshot is taken of the "snap" it is only available for a specific period of time. This is what truly makes it a "moment share".

Omnicore released a statistic stating, "In 2018, Snapchat had an average of 188 million daily active users that generated over three billion snaps a day." That alone proves that millions of users dedicate hours per week to this platform alone.

While it can be a fun app to send messages to your friends, or group of friends, there are some serious security concerns with the app.

Security Dangers of SnapChat

Threats and Other Hateful Language is Deleted

Self-destructing messages have always been a (usually humorous) way to destroy evidence in movies. Yet, the fact that SnapChat deletes messages automatically after a set period of time is the real-life, digital equivalent of the self-destructing message.

While parents should worry about their teens using this and possibly being bullied through the app, adults are under the same threat.

People could be more inclined to send threats and other hurtful information through the app, because the message will be deleted. If the recipient does not take a screenshot of the message, after a small length of time, the snap will no longer be available. This will ensure the sender will get away with it.

Alternatively, you also should not send hurtful or threatening information. Even if it is a joke at the time, if the person saves it, they can use it against you.

Lulls You Into a False Sense of Security

SnapChat, like many other apps often bring users a sense of joy, social connectivity, and belonging. Even though you may not personally know all the people on your friend's list, it is possible to create a bond with people. Since you are interacting with so many people, likely every day, you have a tendency to let your guard down. You start to think of the people on your SnapChat as your friends, even though you have never met. This evokes a trust in these internet friends that might not be warranted (or safe).

Nevertheless, after doing something for a long time, without any hint of danger, the threat level is severely decreased. When this happens, the person, teen or adult, can be lulled into a false sense of security. This false sense of security could cause you to reveal details about your life that you usually would keep off the internet.

Do not fall for this trap. Keep your guard up and while you can enjoy the social scene created by SnapChat do not ever underestimate the potential risk.

Keeping Yourself Protected

SnapChat can be fun, silly, and harmless but it can also be scary. It is not difficult to attract people that might want more from you than a reaction. That is why it is important to be cautious when speaking to people through the app.

Make Sure Your Snap is Safe

Snaps are generally quick pictures. The idea is that the snap takes place like an in-person conversation. Your reaction and response is intended to be immediate. Through that sense for immediacy it is possible that you could send a picture or response that reveals information you might not want to put on the internet. Whether it is something silly, like dirty laundry basket or an important detail from your past, mistakes happen. Most of the time, this could be a fairly safe, as you are generally talking to someone we knew in real life. But, this is not a guarantee. Whether it is a friend of a friend or a complete stranger, it is hard to always know the intentions of the person you are speaking with. If you make a habit out of keeping intensely personal information out of your snaps, it will be less likely that a mistake like this will go to the wrong person.

Keep Your Location OFF

Okay, so this, once again, sounds like a tip that shouldn't have to be stated. After all, most people, adults especially, would agree that they value their privacy. If you look at many SnapChat profiles, though, you would never know it. For many profiles throughout SnapChat, the location is set to ON.

This is so that people can know if there are other SnapChat friends nearby.

As it was stated previously, this is another idea that SnapChat had which sounds great, idealistically, but does not work so well in the real world. On the surface, knowing if your friends are nearby is great. Although, realistically, there are plenty of ways to ask friends if they are nearby without displaying your location information to everyone. Predators are everywhere, unfortunately, no matter what your age or gender. Unlike running into a friend at the grocery store, it only takes one horrific event, where some creep sees your location, to put you in real danger.

So, please, keep your location OFF. If you want to figure out where your friends are, just text them.

Instagram

Instagram is now owned by Facebook, so you can imagine the lack of privacy concerns the platform has. However, that is not the only issue that should have you worried for your personal security while using the photo-prone app.

First, the company who started the Instagram platform was direly understaffed for the amount of attention it received in such a short time period. This meant that the policing of inappropriate content trudged along at a snail's pace. When the company was sold, the new owners seemed to take an 'if it ain't broke, don't fix it' mentality. Still, people continue to upload pictures of themselves and their lives in droves.

Admittedly, Instagram does have a cool premise; not quite as instantaneous as SnapChat, the app is intended for users to upload pictures and short videos of what they are doing on the go. Sadly, hackers and creeps are able to take advantage of this interesting idea and pervert it to mastermind their own sick intentions.

Security Dangers of Instagram

Depression and Negative Body Image

Royal Society for Public Health conducted a survey of almost 1,500 14 to 24 year olds and concluded that Instagram plays a serious, dangerous role in declining mental health in young people.

The study claimed that they found a solid link between depression, anxiety, and negative body image after using Instagram. In fact, this research led officials to say that Instagram was the worst proponent of social-media related mental health issues. This is because Instagram is filled with images of what people categorize as beautiful. That categorization is hurtful, because it causes younger people to feel as though they do not meet these beauty qualifications. This repeated indoctrination of 'beautiful' images eventually leads to people feeling depressed.

It is important to be positive about what is shown on your newsfeed. Understanding that everyone is different is a great start to rise above the urge to compare yourself to others.

On the RSPH's side, they are pushing for 'image-focused' platforms to provide support for heavy users. While it is unclear whether their ideas will be implemented, or if it will work. Still, it is nice to know that somebody is trying to help curb the heavy image-context that is leading to what experts are calling social media psychosis.

Instagram Creeps

Of all the social media platforms, Instagram seems to have the boldest creeps. (Maybe it is because anyone can Directly Message anyone else.) For whatever reason, though, this highly public social media network has plenty of people who will message random strangers for no other reason, but to phish for a response. If these people are answered, even once, there is no telling what could happen. These people could be predators or hackers. The ability to shield your true identity on Instagram is scary and can prove to be dangerous.

Keeping Yourself Protected

Due to the nature of Instagram, it is extremely important to keep yourself protected, both from your own self-doubt and from Instagram creepers. Here are the best ways to keep yourself safe and secure on Instagram.

Use It For Fun

Instagram is an image-related social network. There are plenty of gorgeous, stunning, and interesting pictures. People are not the only focus of the network, so do not focus on what people have to offer. Only follow accounts that interest you. Whether this is makeup, travel, animals, or anything else, make sure you are following people for what they do; not what they look like.

Alternatively, share images that make you smile. If it is a great selfie that you're sharing, more power to you. If it is a beautiful sunset, an adorable picture of your pet, or whatever makes you happy, then that is great too! The point is that you should be able to participate in Instagram because you are enjoying your life not trying to compete with anyone else.

Do Not Respond to Random Messages

It is common for people to get random, weird, and sometimes creepy messages from people on Instagram. Do not respond to these people, because it is just asking for trouble. If someone was genuinely messaging you for a reason, (such as for business, promotion, or because they want to talk to you), they are going to explain that in the message. Usually, one-word messages are simply phishers who want to try to trick you. Responding to them is a major cyber security breach and basically, you do not want to have to deal with it.

Prepare

Protect Your Password

Passwords are a concept that most people understood long before they were required at every turn. However, those passwords were usually a random word and they were meant to be shared with friends in that group. While that is not exclusively outdated, even people within the same organization have their own passwords. Thus, when it comes to any device, organization, or social network that requires a password, you are going to want to protect it. Protecting your password comes in three main tips:

- Don't make your pasword make sense.
- Change Your Password Every 90 Days
- Do NOT Tell Anyone Your Password...Ever!

Be Leery Of Everyone

The scary part about the internet is even if you think you are talking to your best friend, partner, mother, child, or any other trusted person, you can never be sure who is on the other side of the screen. Even though their name and picture might be there, there is no way to truly know if that person is hacked. Thus, it is important to always be cautious of any interaction online. If the person starts asking for obnoxiously personal information, or says that they are in trouble, call that person before giving them that information. Chances are, if they really do need that information or they really are in trouble, they are not going to tell you over social media. Think about it; if you need information or help, is your first thought, *I need to* **message** *my mother (father, sibling, best friend, significant other)!* No. Most people would call the person they want to speak to. If you are messaging them, (not even texting them) it is probably extenuating circumstances. So, be leery if someone does something like that to you.

Check New Profiles

When anyone friend requests you, before you add them, at least check their profile to make sure it wasn't born yesterday. There are plenty of dummy profiles, some with convincing pictures, that literally have that one picture. Even if, by some odd happenstance that isn't a dummy account, you have to ask yourself, why would you, often a stranger, be one of the first people they friend request?

Do Not Add Friends More Than Once

Everyone has gotten the random request from someone they are sure they are friends with already. Regardless of what the person says, if you are already friends with that person, do not add them again. At the very least, ask the profile that you know is them if they were hacked or if they sent another friend request. Although there are always exceptions, more often than not, they will tell you that someone hacked their account.

Delete Creepy Messages

Sure, Instagram is notorious for creepy messages but they can come from any social networking profile. When they come in, it is best to ignore and delete them. If the "person" continues to try to contact you, block them. Unfortunately, we live in a world where you cannot ever let your guard down while online. There are more people out there that will do more harm than good, so you need to be extremely careful. Remember if they are legitimately reaching out to you, they will explain themselves. If it is a generic message, it is probably a scam, hacker, or at the very least a creeper.

So, a good rule when receiving messages or friend/follow requests from people is that if there is something fishy about it, it usually stinks. You don't want to end up finding out you made a mistake after it is too late, so always investigate before you accept anything through social media profiles.

React

Social media is a form of networking and entertainment that most people interact with on a daily basis. People get their news from social media, they keep up with friends, and sometimes, social media is an intricate part of their business. Therefore, it usually doesn't take long for someone to figure out their social media profile is hacked. Nevertheless, it is always better to find out sooner, rather than later. So, here are a few ways you can tell if your profile was hacked.

Posts You DID NOT Create are Added to Your Account

Scammers and hackers often flood their victim's profile with awkward posts. It is usually content that is drastically different than what you normally post (assuming you do not try to hack your friends or sell them any enhancement products). When you notice this, delete these posts right away. This is not only to save yourself embarrassment, it is also to protect your friends. Many of the links posted in hacking posts are doorways that lead to them hacking anyone who clicks on it. Basically, they are using the trust your friends and family have in you to get to their devices. Rude, right?

The List of "People" You Follow Has Risen Significantly

Admittedly, this might be hard to catch at first, because many people follow a lot of different people. Especially with the rise of influencers across platforms, it can be easy for your following list to reach high numbers. However, if you start to notice that you are following a lot of new people and you have no idea who they are, you are probably hacked. Usually, it is the profile posts that give their deception away. Again, the new and unwelcome profiles on your newsfeed will have content that you have no interest in.

You are Logged Out Of Your Profile

If you try to log into your social media account and your password is not working, immediately reset your password. Chances are, a hacker has locked you out and you have to regain control as quickly as possible.

Also, do not change the password back to your original password. That one is already compromised. Instead, pick a completely new password. Also, log out of the social network on all other devices. This will kick them out and make it so they need to hack the new password to get back in.

Secure

Even cybersecurity consensus people can get hacked. If you are hacked, it is nothing to be embarrassed about. The most important thing is to regain control and secure your networks. Yes, this will mean admitting that you were hacked, but it is better than subjecting your unsuspecting friends to the same annoyance. Here is how to secure your accounts after a social media account has gotten hacked:

Change Your Password

This first, crucial tip is to change your password. Even if you are not locked out of your account, if you were hacked, you are not the only person with access to it. Therefore, you need to deny the hacker access as soon as possible. The best way to do that is to change your password, to something completely different, and log out of all other devices.

You will have to put the password in again to get back into the devices you want to have the network attached to, but it is worth it. You want to kick the hacker out as soon as humanly possible.

Delete Any Hacker Posts

Sure. Most of the time, hacker posts are going to be weird and you are going to want them off your page. However, many hacker posts have malicious links that could target your friends. If this is the case, the longer you have these posts on your feed, the more of a chance that a friend will become the hacker's next victim by clicking on the link.

Tell Your Friends

Telling your friends about the hack is not the most comfortable thing you will ever do. Yet, it is necessary and likely, you will be met with sympathy from followers. After all, it is not uncommon to be hacked.

The way that you should tell your friends varies, depending on the severity of the hack. If you catch it in time and no one was contacted, to your knowledge, by the hacker, it is okay to just write a post. If you know certain people were contacted though, it is a good idea to contact them directly and tell them what happened. That way, they can be aware of the situation if anything strange happens on their account.

Change Other Passwords

It is common for people to have one password that is identical or similar, for all of their accounts. If this is the case, you need to assume that the hacker knows what all of your other accounts are from having an admin's view of your network. Therefore, it is important to change all your other passwords too.

Additionally, many hackers gain access to social media profiles through a vulnerable email address. With this in mind, it is important to make sure all your attached emails are secure. It also doesn't hurt to change those passwords, just to be safe; even if they were different then your social media network password.

Chapter 12

INTERNET PROFILES

Internet profiles are becoming extremely more prevalent. It is no surprise that digital means of authorization and esteem are starting to hold internet profiles in high esteem. In fact, in search engine optimization, a method of categorizing the rank of search engines for a certain keyword or phrase, leans heavily on internet profiles. If you cannot prove who you say you are, or what you say you've done, search engines will not give you credit for your hard work and experience.

Usually, though, this is fairly simple. Connecting to the internet profiles of companies you work for, especially being featured on their website as an employee, goes a long way. Yet, depending on your job, your current title, and the unknown intentions of hackers, scammers and thieves, the attention you receive could be life threatening.

Real World Example

This is a scary case because the people targeted thought they were doing something to better their career. They were probably proud of these particular profiles, but instead of helping them get ahead in their occupational endeavors, it caused them to become victims.

In February, 2015, the first of four kidnappings took place. Two armed men took a Connecticut bank executive, Matthew Yussman and his elderly mother hostage. Strapping what the bank executive thought was a bomb to his chest and another under his mother's bed, the bank executive was driven to his bank and instructed to rob it. Under the threat of the bombs being detonated, Yussman did what he was instructed. However, when the police showed up at the bank, the abductors had absconded and the executive was arrested for the crime.

More bank robberies, where family members were threatened would take place in Tennessee, North Carolina, Georgia, and South Carolina.

Ultimately, two ex-cons were convicted of the robberies but it was found out that the vehicle through which the robbers choose their victims were their online profiles. The bank had the profiles of their employees displayed on their website. (Pictures and all.) The thieves would then search through social media profiles to find personal information about their lives and families of their potential victims. (LinkedIn and Facebook were the primary sources of information at this point.) Once the robbers found a mark with enough information, they struck.

The robbers were said to have made off with an estimated $150,000. However, the money has yet to be discovered.

You can learn more about this case here.

Prepare

Do Not Allow Companies to Post Information About You

Sure. This sounds a little weird but if you have a job that deals directly with money or other high-value items, do not get your name and picture posted on the company website. If people are able to match your name to your professional photo, with your job title, they can easily find the information to ruin your life. They can find out about your family, your friends, and even your children. Even if your social network profiles are private, there is someone who is close to you that does not have a private profile. As sad as it is, it does not take a lot of sleuthing to connect the dots. Between your professional and personal networks, along with the unintentional help from your friends, they will be able to gather enough information on you to figure out who to target.

Therefore, the best way to mitigate this, since you cannot control your friends or family, is to ask your company not to share your profile on their website.

Do Not Publicise a Relationship to Anyone Online

Certain social networks, Facebook especially allows users to tag someone as a family member. While, to normal people, this is harmless. After all, you are proud of your family and you want people to know who you belong to. Yet, to a hacker, this is a direct line to what you hold dear. This means, again, even if you are careful about what you post, if a stalker or hacker finds a relationship on a social network, they know they are on the right track.

Do Not Use Your Real Name on Your Social Media Profiles

Surely, everyone has had this experience; they are looking for a friend and their name or "handle" is not their real name. While this can be frustrating at times, it is a good idea, to keep your real name off your social media profiles. Some people use their maiden name while some people use more of a screen name. This way, if someone with malicious intent searches your real name, only professional images and profiles show up. Basically, nothing of importance for someone with malicious intent should show up.

Keep Your Personal and Professional Profiles Separate

This tip links to the previous tip but it is a little bit different. Say you have a LinkedIn profile, you do not want to post a Facebook profile link on your LinkedIn. The first reason this is a bad idea is that you do not want the professional world to find pictures about your personal life. The second reason is that you do not want to go through all the trouble of setting up a screen name for your personal profile, just to link your professional profile right to it. Keep your professional profile and personal profiles as separate as possible.

React

Hopefully, it never gets to this point but if you feel like someone is watching you, you need to react before they make their move. This is a terrifying experience, for sure, but ignoring it is not going to make it go away. So, instead, take these preventative measures to protect yourself.

Do Not React

Reacting, at all, to any threats, messages, or anything else that tips them off that you have received their call for attention is playing into exactly what they want. This is a power trip for them. They want to know you have heard them. Even cursing them out, threatening them back, or simply telling them to leave you alone tells them they have you right where they want you.

File a Police Report

If you suspect someone is watching you, either in person or online, tell the police. Get a record of it and tell them what you know. Most of the time, stalkers and attackers are people that the victim knows. If it is work-related, it is likely someone who has come into your place of business. Even if you don't have a name, making the police aware of what you feel might be going on might be enough to get them to back off. If it isn't enough to stop them, the police will have documentation so if it escalates, they will be apprised of what has happened previously.

Get New Tech

Being watched or stalked is horrifying and inconvenient in so many ways. One of the worse inconveniences though, is having to get new devices. If you believe someone is following you, or stalking you, it is important to ditch your old devices and buy everything new. In this extreme situation, it is not enough to simply change passwords. In this situation, it is best to get brand new devices. The reason being, you can't be sure if the hacker has installed spyware on your devices. The only surefire way to know you are safe, is to get new devices.

Secure

This is a little different, as it is more about being safe and returning to your normal life, than simply adding some antivirus software to a device. Hopefully, this never, ever happens to you but if it does, this is the best way to secure your life, or the life of someone close to you.

Do What You Are Told

If you or a loved one is being threatened by a hacker, stalker, robber, kidnapper, or other type of criminal, it is best to do what you are told. Stay calm and get the most information you possibly can out of them. Try to listen for clues but do not ask where they are or where the loved one is. Ultimately, let the criminals call the shots. According to The Conversation, 97% of kidnappings are resolved without the victim being hurt. The three percent that do end badly are usually due to the victim trying to escape or a pre-existing medical condition attacking the victim.

Do Not Call the Police, Right Away

"No police," is a saying that is repeated over and over in movies, books, and in real life kidnapping situations. Obviously, the criminal does not want the police to be called. However, is there a possibility that the victim does not want the police to be called as well?

KidGuard advises parents NOT to call the police; at least, not at first. Instead, the company advises that the victim's family calls a private security firm. Their rationale is that police are going to want to get the criminal, while the first priority of the private security firm will want to get the victim returned safe.

There are a few potential problems with this, though:

- The police (FBI especially) have a plethora of resources and according to kidnapping statistics, if the victim survived the abduction, they are probably going to be okay. So, calling the police is likely still the best move.

- Eventually, the police are going to get involved, whether you call them or not. Once that happens, the victim's family is going to look pretty suspicious. The first question the police are going to ask is why you didn't call them and telling them your suspicions on their priorities will not go over well.

Nevertheless, they do have a point, so let's hope that no one reading this actually has to worry about making this awful decision.

Do Not Give into Emotion

Stay calm, of course. This was already covered and it is far easier said than done in this situation. Although, there will be another emotion that will likely be screaming at you to come out, regardless of how calm you are: The urge to give them anything they want. For most people, their family and friends are priceless. Thus, most people would be willing to do anything they possibly could to get their loved ones back safely. The problem is that if you give into your emotion and tell them how much you are willing to give them, they will likely keep going higher. If you agree to truly give them anything they want, that sets a precedence.

One famous kidnapping case happened in 1973, when John Paul Getty III was kidnapped. His grandfather, oil tycoon (and billionaire) J. Paul Getty originally refused to pay the ransom, telling the media, "I don't believe in paying kidnappers. I have 14 other grandchildren and if I pay one penny now, then I'll have 14 kidnapped grandchildren."

While this is a seemingly unbelievable statement, this is sort of what this tip means. If you give in immediately and give them whatever they want, you could be putting everyone you know in peril.

Virtual Kidnapping

Over the past twenty years, Virtual Kidnapping has become a scam that has improved greatly in its horrific level of believability. Virtual Kidnapping is when the hackers are able to "spoof" the number of a victim's loved one. This "spoofing" makes it appear as though the person is calling from their loved-one's phone. Through social media, the hacker learns about the relationship of the victim to the chosen loved one and goes to work. When the hacker calls the victim, they claim that they have kidnapped their loved one. They threaten to hurt or kill the loved one, if a certain amount is not paid.

This happens surprisingly often, with a cluster of the hackers originating from Venezuela. Unfortunately, there is not much that can be done about this, since it is out of police jurisdiction and they did not actually kidnap anyone. However, that does not mean that it is any less harrowing for the person who gets that horrible call.

What to do if you receive a call like this?

The first thing you need to do is get in touch with the threatened loved one, while keeping the hacker on the phone. Once you make sure your loved one is safe, you can hang up. They hold no power over you, after you are sure your loved one is not in danger.

The only good news is that when a phone is "spoofed" it is not taken over. The person whose device was spoofed can still work their phone normally. So, you should be able to get in touch with them normally, as they are hopefully not in any danger.

However, the authorities urge you to report the call, as police are trying to build a case so that one day they will be able to end this terrible form of attempted extortion.

Chapter 13

THIRD-PARTY HACKS

Unfortunately, because of all the different networks, logins, and capabilities of the internet, we are never completely in control of our information. Even if you are extremely careful about where you put your information, you are still vulnerable to an attack on many third-party hacks.

Usually, these hacks are widely-known and end in some kind of class action suit. However, money can only buy so much privacy and if your information is compromised there is no way to go back in time. Once the hackers have the information, they have it.

Real Life Example

This breach has been going on for quite a while. In 2017, Experiean finally admitted that they realized they were breached. The company that is supposed to be responsible with our credit information is literally the glass house that throws stones each time anyone applies for a loan. They messed up royally and yet, they are still on top of the credit world. Their reaction to this breach was a public relations nightmare that took two years to find some semblance of a conclusion. The payout for damages has totaled up to 650 million dollars, according to KrebsonSecurity.

While that sounds like a lot of money, the number of people who were affected by this data breach is estimated to be 148 million. When you look at it that way, the figure is relative.

Thankfully, there are ways that you can stay protected from data breaches like this, even if it is the fault of a third-party. Taking precautions to protect yourself can always minimize the impact of data breaches like this one.

Also, do not be fooled. Even though this data breach is massive and the company handled it so horribly that the security of their website is still in question, this danger is not exclusive to credit companies. A third-party breach can happen through your bank, your credit card company, stores you shop at, or websites you frequent. Unfortunately, companies are vulnerable to hacks, just like an individual is vulnerable.

Thus, if this hack with Experience has taught us nothing else, know that the only one who can and will look out for your cybersecurity and wellbeing is you. Never rely on third parties, regardless of how *secure* they claim to be, to maintain your cybersecurity.

Prepare

Monitor Your Credit Score

For many adults, checking their credit score evokes the same feeling that you would get when getting a test back. Some people sit in the front of the class and they look forward to getting their test back. Some are on the edge and could be happy or horrified at the result. Then, there are those who in the back of the class and hope to anything and everything that is holy that they pass at all.

Regardless of where you sit in this proverbial class, monitoring your credit score is a key element to your cybersecurity. Knowing what is going on is paramount to making sure no one is messing around with your identity.

There are many different avenues through which you can check your credit on a weekly or monthly basis. Credit Karma is one of the most popular but certain lines of credit also monitor your credit score for you.

Set Up Credit Fraud Alerts

Setting up credit fraud alerts can be set up to send a text, phone-call, or email to you whenever your credit is accessed. This could be when your credit card is used or if someone applies for a line of credit with your information. Getting these types of alerts can help you rest assured that you are not being taken advantage of. These alerts do not always stop identity theft, but it does help people head it off at the pass.

If a fraudulent charge or application is posted against your credit, the sooner it is reported, the sooner you can rectify the situation. Thus, if you receive an alert you do not recognize, make sure you get to the bottom of it right away. The longer you wait, the more difficult it will be to get your money back and/or get the fraudulent activity expunged from your record.

Keep a Close Eye On When and Where You Use Your Credit Cards

When people are used to using their credit cards for most purchases, it is incredibly easy to just swipe it now and settle the damages at the end of the month when the bill is due. While using credit cards and paying them off is a good way to help your credit every month, the swipe now, pay later method is not the most secure.

It is important to keep track of where you swipe your card and when. That way, if your card is compromised, it will be easier to pick out a purchase that you didn't make. (Often, credit card scammers make a small purchase, to see if the victim notices, before making any large purchases.)

Thankfully, online statements and apps dedicated to credit lines will tell you which purchases were made with your card in minutes; whether it was you or not. With that knowledge, it is important to check these transactions regularly.

Passwords Are Really Important Here

Passwords are not the best form of protection against cyber threats but a well curated password can help keep you safe. The harder it is for a hacker to break into your account, the safer you are and passwords are like locked doors. If you have a good password, it is more of a deadbolt than a chintzy run of the mill lock. It is possible to get inside but they are going to have to do better than sliding a credit card inside the door.

Signs of Credit Fraud

If you take anything away from this book let it be that you are responsible for your own cybersecurity. No one is going to do it for you. No person or company realistically can do it for you. Therefore, you need to keep a watchful eye out for the signs and make sure that you keep control over your own security.

Here are a few little-known signs that your credit is being hacked:

Bills Stop Coming to your Home

No one likes bills. Going to the mailbox and finding out you owe a company money is never the most pleasant realization. Yet, unless you have found a way to be completely self-sufficient, monthly bills are a reality. So, if bills stop coming to your home, you are going to want to investigate. Chances are, someone is not paying those bills for you, so there must be something wrong.

The most likely reason for the lack of mail is that the hacker has changed your billing address. (Still, the hacker is not paying your bills. Sorry.)

Your Tax Refund is Denied

You can mess with credit. You can steal the money out of our bank, but when you mess with the big, beautiful check that is our tax refund, it's war!

Seriously, though, many people rely on their tax refund to help them get ahead, save, or purchase annual necessities. Besides, you are entitled to that money, so it doesn't matter what you do with it, you deserve to receive that check.

If you have done everything you are supposed to do and your refund is denied, that is scary. Having any issues with the IRS can be difficult but that is one terrible way to find out you have been hacked.

The main reason this would happen is if someone submits your taxes and collects your check before you do. That would mean, they would need to know your social security number and that is another scary realization.

React

When it comes to credit fraud, the sooner you react, the better. If you suspect credit card fraud, it is important to take the proper precautions to protect yourself. Here are the best steps you can take to react to any suspicious activity.

Get Copies of Your Credit Reports

While monitoring your credit is important, when there is suspicion of fraud it is necessary that you receive a copy of your credit report. The FACT Act entitles you to receive an annual copy of your credit report from all three agencies. That means, you should be able to get a free, complete credit report every year.

If you are in need of a credit report more than once or twice a year, you are likely more compromised than you realize. It might be a good idea to invest in continual credit monitoring services.

Inform all Financial Institutions

If you are afraid something has gone awry with your credit, it is pertinent that you inform all of your financial institutions. Telling your bank and credit card companies about the possible breach can save you a lot of time and aggravation. Credit companies and financial institutions understand the risks and they want to help keep their customers safe. (It is in the company's best interest. If their customers are safe, they keep their cards and the company keeps getting paid.)

Keep your financial institutions informed. This will always work out better for you in the long run.

Secure

Freeze Your Credit

What does it mean to freeze your credit? According to Consumer Finance, freezing credit means to disallows creditors from accessing your credit reporting file. When creditors cannot access this file, they cannot offer you credit. This bars identity thieves from opening accounts in your name.

Oddly enough, it is not as harrowing an experience as it sounds and it is extremely beneficial for those that are afraid they were hacked.

A Federal Law that was passed in September of 2018 declares that you are allowed to freeze and unfreeze your credit for free. The only mandate is that each of the three credit report agencies, Transunion, Equifax, and Experian are all contacted individually.

This law grants people a lot more freedom over their credit report file and helps them get back on track after a breach.

During a credit freeze the only entities that are allowed to access your credit report profile are your current credit providers, companies that you hire to keep track of your credit, and certain government entities. Everyone else is completely barred.

Continue Monitoring Your Credit Report for 90 Days

Mobile devices can sometimes be corrupted by a single app that is placed on the phone. In some cases, when that app is deleted, the phone is cured. While it sounds easy, this could be a more harrowing process than you might originally think. Most people have a lot of apps on their phones. Even moderately cyber-security conscientious people fall for downloading apps on a whim. While most of the time it is fine, sometimes, you download a diseased app.

Report Any Strange Activity on Your Credit Report Immediately

While you are monitoring your credit, it is extremely important to take action if you notice anything suspicious. This time period is crucial, because if something does happen and you do not catch it immediately, it might take a month to show up on your credit report. That means that by the time you realize something is amiss, it has already been a month. The good news is, credit companies are well aware of this and if you report it as soon as you see it, there is a good chance you can catch it in time.

Get New Credit Cards

Although this is a real hassle, in some situations, it is important to get new credit cards. The only good thing about this is that most financial institutions will issue a new card, with a new number, without much difficulty. It is also, usually, free.

The most frustrating parts of this process are waiting for the new cards to come in, using temporary cards, and switching all your payment information. If you are not a person who saves payment information for monthly withdraw, this can be easier than it is for most. Yet, there are many different companies now that keep a payment on file and it can mess up your subscription if the card is no longer active.

Chapter 14

PUBLIC WIFI

Coffee shops. Airplane terminals. Bus stations. Train stations. Internet Cafes (yes, they still exist).

These are all places that are known for having public WiFi. Of course, there are plenty of other places that have public wifi, but these are the most common. While enjoying the true artisan experience or killing time online while waiting for public transportation is not wrong, it does put you at a greater risk.

Public Wifi is, obviously, public. That means that there are multiple people and devices connecting to one network at any given time. For a hacker, this is a digital smorgasbord.

Here is how you can keep yourself safe, while enjoying the freedom of working on the go.

Prepare

Connect to Trusted Networks

While it is never ideal to connect to Public WiFi, sometimes you need to or you want to. Whatever the reason you find yourself going against your better judgement, *at least* connect to a trusted network. Most places, whether it is a coffee shop or public transportation, have their own network available. This network should be identifiable by their network name.

While it isn't guaranteed protection, it is much better than latching on to some random network and exposing your information to who knows what. If you are going to connect to a Public Wifi network, at least be sure you know that you are dealing with a trusted, reputable entity, at least.

Configure the Settings and Turn Off Sharing

When accessing most WiFi networks, a popup will ask if this is a public network. It is at this time that you need to configure the network settings so that Sharing is Turned OFF. While this seems like a no-brainer, it is astonishing how many people bypass this safety precaution.

Visit Websites that are Secured with HTTPS

HTTP and HTTPS are the start of a website that many people do not even pay attention to. Normally, that is okay but when you are trying to be secure in a naturally vulnerable digital environment, you need to pay attention. Using Https sites mean that there is a level of security automatically fused into the website. Therefore, there is a layer of protection between your information and lurking hackers.

Use a VPN

While using a VPN at home is a good way to ensure you are protected, using a VPN when accessing Public WiFi is practically common sense. This will give you, specifically a level of protection that encrypts your data. Therefore, you can feel safer doing whatever it is that you need to do online. With a VPN, you do not have to worry that you are completely exposing yourself to everyone else who is sharing the network.

Mind Your Browsing Habits

When you are using a Public WiFi network, it is important to be conscientious of what you are accessing. If you are typing in passwords and other sensitive information, you are much more likely to be compromised if there is a hacker "sharing" the network.

To be safe, regardless of taking previous precautions, you should stay away from the following online activities during your time on a Public WiFi Network:

- Banking
- Online Shopping

- Payment Transactions
- Logging into Work-Related Databases
- Accessing Other Sensitive Information

React

Always Log Out

Log out of everything once you are done using it on a Public WiFi Network, even if it is a network you trust. Remember, when you are using trusted Public WiFi, it isn't the owner of the network you necessarily need to worry about, it's the other patrons using the same network. Therefore, it is important to always log out of everything, even if you are still using the network. Are you checking your email, do not leave the tab open while you do other things. It can be a port of entry for a hacker. The same goes for social networks and anything else were you have an account. Whenever you are done, make sure you log out.

Use Your Cellular Hotspot Instead of Free WiFi

Most people forget they even have a hotspot available on their mobile devices. The reason being is that it is usually not as fast or convenient as a regular WiFi connection. It is sure better than getting hacked, though. If you have this option, this is a great way to add a level of protection that a Public WiFi network can't give you.

Log Into Your Internet Provider

Xfinity is a big proponent of this nifty feature but other companies provide it as well. Instead of using a Public WiFi connection, check to see if your internet provider will connect in that area. If it does, you should be able to log in to your home connection and use that. This is an extremely safe option, as you are getting the privacy and security that you would from your home internet connection.

Secure

Change Your Passwords

If you are using a Public WiFi and you think you are getting or have gotten hacked, disconnect from the network immediately and change the passwords. Ideally, you want to change all of your passwords but if you want to be quick about it, definitely change the passwords of the places you visited while on the network.

Shut Off Your Computer

Shutting off your computer will ensure the virus cannot spread. When you get home, do a malware check and see if anything comes up. Even after the check, though, it is important that you keep an eye on the way your computer is running. If it starts to act weird, or you start receiving strange messages/emails, you may have to wipe the drive.

Chapter 15

PASSWORDS

Ah, passwords. For some of us, they are the bane of our existence. While, alternatively, others take pride in being able to remember a long, drawn-out password that looks more like hyroglifics than your native language. Now, with the incessant need to log into EVERYTHING, passwords are a part of our daily life. People need them to get into their mobile devices, their computers, their social networks, and their work systems. It is ridiculous but it does keep unwanted people from stealing your information in a crime of opportunity.

Unfortunately, passwords are a lot like the lock on your front door. It doesn't take much to crack, decrypt, or even completely bypass a password, especially if the network is not effectively protected. That is a scary thought but it is a reality that we must come to grips with, if we are going to have a productive conversation about cybersecurity.

Nevertheless, passwords are still a helpful deterrent and therefore, should be used to the full extent of their protective capabilities.

Real World Example

There are so many passwords hacked per day, that the singular real-world example does not work here. In fact, according to Tripwire, passwords can be bought for $1 on the Black Market. That is almost insulting.

Yet, the real reason that passwords are bought, sold, and traded so easily is that humans are predictable. (Sorry.) There are many different 'techniques' that hackers use to guess passwords and some of the tricks are older than the internet.

According to CNN, even in 2019, the list of the top ten most popular passwords makes those in cybersecurity shudder:

1. 123456
2. 123456789
3. qwerty
4. Password
5. 111111
6. 12345678
7. Abc123
8. 1234567
9. Password1
10. 12345

For supposedly being at the top of the food chain, this is pathetic. This isn't a list from 2000 or 2010. This is a list from 2019! Year after year, this list is composed and guess what? Year after year, the top ten passwords are pretty much the same!

People seem to think that hackers are so smart (and they would like you to believe they are) but in reality, we as a society just can't part with the dumbest passwords ever. If you're thinking that it is so dumb, nobody would guess it, you're wrong.

Basically, if your password is on this list, do not read any further. Please, just go change it and come back when it is literally anything else.

Prepare

Change Your Password every 90 Days

Yes. It is a pain but again, it is more convenient than being hacked and having to explain to grandma that you didn't really send her that porno link. Think of it like any other ritualistic habit you have. Set it on the calendar and change it when the 90-day mark comes.

Elongate Your Passwords

Remember, to a computer, every key is basically a selection of ones and zeros. As far as a computer password is concerned, the linguistic complexity is far less important than the length. The good news is, you don't have to bother with trying to remember where that dollar sign goes or how many hashtags you put in this particular password. Instead, make your passwords long, not complex.

The More Nonsensical the Password the Better

More often than not, it is the "human factor" that is exploited by hackers when they attempt to guess passwords. We all do it. We want a password that we are going to remember, so we usually choose something that is important to us. (Our child's name or birthdate, an anniversary, your spouse's name or the name of a beloved pet.) Unfortunately for your trip down memory lane, most of that information is probably on your social media profiles. Thus, it is more of a game to hackers than a precaution.

Instead, use a phrase that makes no sense. Sure, it might be more difficult for you to remember but it is safer.

React

Keep Your Password Off Your Desk (And Devices)

This sounds logical but after you decide on a password, there are so many people that make the mistake of writing the password down somewhere obvious, it's ridiculous. For example, if you followed the tips to creating a secure password and you write it down on your desk, don't you think a random phrase is going to catch someone's attention? Better yet, people put their passwords on their device, often under the contacts. Again, if someone sees your phone contacts, it will likely be easy to pick out which contact is your password. (Also, if you feel you must do this, DO NOT name the contact "Password". Please.)

Don't Give Your Password Out

There are very few genuine reasons to give out your password to anyone. Even if that person is super trustworthy, things happen. Plus, the more people you tell, the higher the possibility that it will get into the wrong hands.

Also, if your password does get out, change it immediately. No one else has any business being able to access your private login information.

Secure

Change Your Password

In the event that you do get hacked, it is important to change your password and kick everyone else out. That means you will have to log in again on your devices, yes, but if there is a threat, this step will boot them out.

One other thing, do not make your new password similar to your old password. That is just asking for trouble.

Scan Your Computer

By now, you should know the drill. Scan your computer for malware and keep an eye out for anything suspicious, even if the scan comes back clean. Sometimes, malware can be dormant until it starts to corrupt your device. Even then, you might have to rely on strange clues to tell you that you are hacked.

Chapter 16

VPNS

A Virtual Private Network (VPN) encrypts the data going in and out of your network. It will hide all of the IP information from prying eyes and it disallows your Internet Service Provider (ISP) to see what you are accessing online. Basically, it is an effective cloak of invisibility for your data and web surfing.

People sometimes associate the use of VPNs strictly with the use of Tor. However, VPNs stretch far beyond the Tor Network. Hiding your IP address and encrypting the data is a smart way to protect yourself from many threats lurking in emails and throughout the web. Plus, it helps to keep your information private.

VPN FAQ

VPNs and their worth could come across as somewhat elusive in their description. So, to try to clear up the description and purpose for VPNs, here are some Frequently Asked QUestions, with regard to this safety precaution:

Do VPNs protect against Viruses and Trojans?

Unfortunately, no. VPNs only encrypt your data and the traffic that goes in and out of your network. Think of it like a filtration system. However, **malware** and **antivirus** can protect against viruses and Trojans. So, again, it is important to keep those security protocols up to date at all times!

Does using a VPN slow down my connection?

The short answer: Yes, but there is a good reason for it. A VPN is like a bouncer, deciding what gets in (and out) of your network. It ensures that everything reaching your protected network is safe and it requires that everything leaving your network is unable to compromise you. This process is encryption. Thus, it makes sense that the data coming and going from your protected network is going to be slowed down.

Although, if the VPN is working properly, the decrease in speed should be so minimal, you won't even notice it. So, do not let the milliseconds of speed you lose sway you against protecting yourself with a VPN.

Can search engines track my browsing with a VPN?

Using a VPN does not absolve you from being targeted with ads that are unique to your searches. However, a VPN effectively hides your IP address from search engines. Instead of revealing your personal IP address, your VPN provider will show the search engine one of their IP addresses, allowing you to browse safely.

Perceived Problems with Encryption

Encrypting devices, much like putting an outdoor lock on an internal door. Sure, it makes it harder to get into but it is also far more noticeable. After all, no one puts a heavy-duty lock on a door with nothing of value behind it. Therefore, encrypting your devices could make you a target because it makes your specific IoT stand out.

The hacker could find your network more attractive because they believe it is encrypted for a reason, or they could simply want a challenge.

This isn't Oceans Eleven. Humans love a challenge and they love to stroke their own ego. Motives are usually far less complicated than the movies. Unfortunately, the movies make it seem far more complicated than it is to be a hacker.

This means that if you are the only encrypted network in their current hacking radar, they could want a challenge. Then, when they do hack into your system, they could be angry that you aren't hiding the

Hope Diamond, they might retaliate by ruining your life.

So, Why Bother Encrypting Devices?

Fortunately, the security encryption that most VPN companies (read:any company worth investing in) is going to be using 256-bit AES encryption. While it *is* hackable, if done correctly, it will take most hackers years to get into such a system. According to Data Motion, unless the hacker knows there is something of value behind this encryption, they won't even try. (But, remember, humans like a challenge.)

The good news is that if someone is specifically targeting your network, the protection of a VPN is going to keep you secure. The bad news is that any VPN isn't an impenetrable shield. While your network is usually safe, any outside, third-party accounts, (bank accounts, Paypal, social media, and even email, in some cases) is still at risk.

How much is a VPN?

VPNs are not expensive. In fact, they are extremely affordable, especially considering the level of encryption they provide. The best VPNs on the market range from $70 to $100 for the first year. Although, many have two and three year plans that protect you for a marginal difference in the annual price. (Some, the difference is less than $10!)

WARNING!

There are free VPN "services" out there and they are available BUT they are not secure. In fact, having a free VPN is more likely to make you a target than protect you from anything. The encryption they provide is minimal and hackers can spot it from across the web. So, please, NEVER, NEVER, NEVER use a free VPN.

What are some of the best VPNs?

1. Nord VPN
2. Express VPN

3. SurfShark
4. Private VPN
5. CyberGhost

Chapter 17

TOR

Tor, The Tor Network, or the extremely rare explanation of its acronym, "The Onion Router" has become synonymous with accessing unsavory portions of the web. Although, there is much more to Tor then what it is iconically used for. Tor, with the help of a VPN can add an extra layer of security and anonymity to your online exploits. This level of protection is also dedicated to making the internet uncensored.

Believe it or not, Tor is actually run by volunteers, with the goal of making internet browsing anonymous. Tor is a product of FireFox, although, many different versions are available.

What does Tor do?

Tor disguises a user's identity by routing information through multiple nodes, which encrypt the information many times before it is delivered to its intended target. That way, the sender (and receiver, if they are using similar precautions) remain anonymous.

Is Tor legal?

Yes. It is legal to use Tor. However, Tor does host illegal content and therefore, it is often the object of scrutiny. Again, most of the time, when people talk about Tor, outside of the realm of cybersecurity, they are talking about using it as a vehicle to access unsavory websites. Yet, that is all Tor is: a vehicle. It is not intended for being used for nefarious purposes. However, the nature of an anonymous router, which defends against censorship does attract shady users. Basically anything that is not indexed in search engines (because of its illegality) is available through Tor.

Yet, Tor was initially created for regular people to salvage their privacy online.

Is Tor completely anonymous?

Using Tor gives users the ability to protect their identity. However, there have been occasions when portions of Tor have been compromised but those issues are fixed quickly. The only real vulnerable spot in Tor is the Exit Node, because that is the last line of defense. It is possible to hack anonymity through this exit node if it is unprotected but that is where a VPN steps in.

Chapter 18

INDEX

Adware: Adware is a type of malware that displays unwanted advertisements ad nauseam. While we can all agree that most ads are not welcomed internet content, this is a malicious attack of ads. Often Adware disallows the victim to even use the computer because of all the ads that pop up.

Bots and Botnets: Bots and Botnets are derived from the word robots. Often, they are designed to handle monotonous tasks. Yet, when they are created by hackers they are usually a bend of worms and viruses, that often help hackers steal their victim's identity.

Computer Virus: A Computer Virus is a malicious software that infects a device. It is designed to self-replicate and is always created by a human. However, after it is released, it is self-sufficient. Humans create computer viruses. Computers do not just get "sick" on their own.

Firewall: A firewall is a cybersecurity feature that allows outside communication but blocks unauthorized access.

- Packet Filters- This firewall controls the network access. This is done by the firewall constantly analyzing the outgoing and incoming packets.
  - "Packets" or Blocks are data that is checked against previously whitelisted data. Examples of this whitelisted data are trusted IP addresses, information nodes, programs and other pre-approved information.

- Stateful Inspection (SPI)- This is a more protected firewall, which examines traffic streams from start to finish. Instead of simply looking for similarities new data, comparable to pre-approved data, this firewall analyzes the packets thoroughly, and provides proxy services.

- Proxy Server Firewalls: These firewalls are the strongest and are usually reserved for bigger networks. These firewalls inspect incoming data at the application layer. Plus, Proxy firewalls are able to hide your IP address, which makes it easier to limit the types of traffic that even attempt to enter the network.

Freeware: Freeware is software that is available to download for free. In the cybersecurity space, there is a limited amount of "freeware" that is actually going to do anything for you. Sometimes, it might even make you a bigger, better target for hackers. However, the one freeware that does help with cybersecurity are the Secure Disk Erase Utilities.

Malware: Malware is any type of software that is designed to harm, disrupt, or gain unauthorized access to a computer system or device. The most common types of malware include:

Keylogger: Keyloggers, sometimes referred to as a keystroke logger is a surveillance malware. This type of malware records everything that is typed into the computer This includes, but is not limited to:

- Passwords
- Account Numbers
- User Names
- Encryption Codes

Keyloggers are found in both mobile and desktop devices.

Rootkit: Rootkit software allows the hacker to access otherwise inaccessible portions of the infected device.

Trojan: A Trojan is a type of computer virus that is designed to look innocent. However, once it gains access to the device, it wreaks havoc on the system.

Worm: Worms, along with Viruses are the most common form of malicious software. A worm works much like a virus, with the same basic abilities. However, a worm does not need a host file. Instead, it can work self-sufficiently, which can make it harder to detect and eradicate.

Spyware: Spyware is software that allows the hacker to retrieve otherwise inaccessible information about their target's computer. The collected information is secretly transmitted back to the hacker via the compromised computer's hard drive.

Operating System (OS): A devices Operating System is the software that allows the device to run its basic functions. Without an OS the device would not be able to do anything, from menial tasks to more advanced operations.

Internet of Things (IoT): "The networking capability that allows information to be sent to and received from objects and devices (such as fixtures and kitchen appliances) using the Internet."- *Webster's Dictionary*

To simplify and explain that a little more succinctly, IoT is the interconnected devices and appliances within a network.

Internet of Everything (IoE): IoE is in completion, all that is considered IoT, in addition to the data that those "things" collect. It is not synonymous with IoT, because it encompasses the interconnected devices and appliances (things) within a network, as well as the information that is gathered through those things.

Tor: Tor, The Tor Network, or the extremely rare explanation of its acronym, "The Onion Router" can add an extra layer of security and anonymity to your online exploits. This level of protection is also dedicated to making the internet uncensored.

Node: A Node is a device or data point that is part of a larger network. This specific connection point represents a point of connection, redistribution, or communication. Specifically relating to cybersecurity a Node is linked to Tor, as in an Exit Node, or the point where the network ends.

Social Media: Social media is a collection of websites and applications (used on both desktop and mobile devices) through which users create, share, and interact with content and other content creators. Social media, for the most part, is used for social networking. Some of the most popular social networks are:

- Facebook
- Twitter
- Instagram

Public Wifi: Public WiFi is often found in public places, such as coffee shops, transportation hubs, and some stores. This is a hotspot network that allows you to access the internet for free. Sadly, Public WiFi Networks make users vulnerable to cyber attacks.

Virtual Private Network (VPN): VPNs are a method of securing your computer via encryption while browsing the internet.

Search Engine Optimization(SEO): SEO is the process, usually enacted by marketers of ensuring a particular website ranks high on search engines such as:

- Google
- Bing
- Yahoo

Voice Assistant: A voice assistant is a digital assistant. Many devices are equipped with voice assistants, which use a combination of natural language processing and speech synthesis to answer the users questions or provide them with the desired information. Here are a few of the most popular Voice Assistants:

- Google
- Alexa
- Seri
- Jarvis (Yes, technically, this is a fictional voice assistant but who doesn't love Jarvis?)